W9-BTL-684

Advance Praise for
CRACKING YOUR RETIREMENT NEST EGG
(WITHOUT SCRAMBLING YOUR FINANCES)
by Margaret A. Malaspina

"For investors who are counting down to retirement, *Cracking Your Retirement Nest Egg* will help them manage what they own—both right now and through their retirement income years."

PETER S. LYNCH
Vice Chairman
Fidelity Management & Research Company

"Peggy Malaspina has done it again! *Cracking Your Retirement Nest Egg* **OFFERS SOOTHING, SENSIBLE, AND REASSURING ADVICE THAT'S JUST RIGHT FOR THESE TURBULENT FINANCIAL TIMES.** Anyone who is worried about making it through (and enjoying) retirement will profit from her step-by-step guide to creating a plan that works. **WHETHER YOU ARE ALREADY RETIRED, PLANNING FOR THE BIG LEAP, OR SIMPLY TRYING TO EASE A PARENT'S FEAR OF BECOMING A FINANCIAL BURDEN AND 'DYING BROKE,' MALASPINA'S BOOK IS THE ONE TO CHOOSE.**"

GINGER APPLEGARTH, CFP, CLU, CHFC
Author, *The Money Diet* and *Wake Up and Smell the Money*

"Margaret Malaspina's command of the retirement landscape and her practical advice for individual participants is delivered in clear, concise, compelling language that anyone can and will relate to. Readers of this book will be reminded about the value of participating in such plans as well as how to do so wisely and well. **THIS BOOK DELIVERS WHAT EVERY INVESTOR IS ALWAYS PINING FOR**—an advantage that will trump mere guesswork. **IT'S AN ESSENTIAL PIECE OF THE PUZZLE FOR ACHIEVING A SECURE FINANCIAL RETIREMENT.**"

JIM LOWELL
Editor
Fidelity Investor

Cracking Your Retirement Nest Egg
(Without Scrambling Your Finances)

Also available from
BLOOMBERG PRESS

Investing in REITs: Real Estate Investment Trusts,
Revised and Updated Edition
by Ralph L. Block

The Business Owner's Guide to Personal Finance:
When Your Business is Your Paycheck
by Jill Andresky Fraser

Wall Street Secrets for Tax-Efficient Investing:
From Tax Pain to Investment Gain
by Robert N. Gordon with Jan M. Rosen

Investing in Small-Cap Stocks, Revised Edition
by Christopher Graja and Elizabeth Ungar, Ph.D.

Plan Now or Pay Later:
Judge Jane's No-Nonsense Guide to Estate Planning
by Jane B. Lucal

Investing in Hedge Funds: Strategies for the New Marketplace
by Joseph G. Nicholas

Stock Options: Getting Your Share of the Action
Negotiating Shares and Terms in
Incentive and Nonqualified Plans
by Tom Taulli

A complete list of our titles is available at
WWW.BLOOMBERG.COM/BOOKS

Cracking Your Retirement Nest Egg

(Without Scrambling Your Finances)

25 Things You Must Know
Before You Tap Your 401(k), IRA,
or Other Retirement Savings Plan

MARGARET A. MALASPINA

BLOOMBERG PRESS
PRINCETON

Books are available for bulk purchases at special discounts. Special editions or book excerpts can also be created to specifications. For information, please write: Special Markets Department, Bloomberg Press.

This publication contains the author's opinions and is designed to provide accurate and authoritative information. It is sold with the understanding that the author, publisher, and Bloomberg L.P. are not engaged in rendering legal, accounting, investment-planning, or other professional advice. The reader should seek the services of a qualified professional for such advice; the author, publisher, and Bloomberg L.P. cannot be held responsible for any loss incurred as a result of specific investments or planning decisions made by the reader.

First edition published 2003
1 3 5 7 9 10 8 6 4 2

Library of Congress Cataloging-in-Publication Data

Malaspina, Margaret A.
    Cracking your retirement nest egg (without scrambling your finances) : 25 things you must know before you tap your 401(k), ira, or other retirement savings plan / Margaret A. Malaspina.
        p. cm.
Includes index.
    ISBN 1-57660-126-9 (alk. paper)
    1. Pension trusts—United States. 2. Pension trusts—Taxation—United States. 3. Pension trusts—Law and legislation—United States. 4. Old age pensions—United States. 5. Old age pensions—Taxation—United States. 6. Old age pensions—Law and legislation—United States. 7. Social security—United States. 8. Retirement income—United States. 9. Finance, Personal—United States. I. Title: 25 things you must know before you tap your 401(k), ira, or other retirement savings plan. II. Title: Twenty five things you must know before you tap your 401(k), ira, or other retirement savings plan. III. Title.

HD7105.45.U6 M32 2003
332.024'01—dc21   2002013470

Edited by Christine Miles

Book design by Don Morris Design

For Derrick

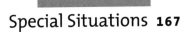

Special Situations 167

ACKNOWLEDGMENTS

IF I HAVE SUCCEEDED in making the transition from retirement savings to retirement income a little easier for my readers, it is because I have had the benefit of talented, knowledgeable, interested associates who have been generous with their time and their ideas.

I especially appreciate the efforts of editors par excellence Jared Kieling and Chris Miles at Bloomberg, for their help, their patience, and their astute advice. I am also indebted to their many Bloomberg associates, including Lisa Goetz, Tracy Tait, Andrew Feldman, and Gail Whiteside, whose collective efforts are proof that an author alone does not a book make. That point was certainly brought home in the production and quality control process, where the expertise of Barbara Diez and her associates, JoAnne Kanaval, Mary Macher, and Maris Williams were greatly appreciated.

Special thanks to the many financial, tax, retirement, and estate planning experts who were willing to answer my questions and review my copy, including Lou Beckerman, John Begley, Kenneth Brier, Farrell Dolan, John Doyle, David Foster, Elizabeth Geiler, Tom Hohl, Deena Katz, John LeBlanc, Marcia Mantell, Seth Medalie, Steve Mitchell, Deborah Novotny, Norman Posner, Ed Slott, and Randy Smith.

This book would not have been completed without the help of my associates at Malaspina Communications—Karen Perkuhn, Nancy Scarlata, and Doug McCusker—who compiled research, checked facts, and made significant contributions to the content of *Cracking Your Retirement Nest Egg*. I can't say "thank you" enough times to cover all that they did during the months this book was in progress.

Thanks to my family for putting up with my deadlines and late nights—to my children, Elizabeth and Peter, and to Derrick, my partner in life and at the bridge table. You're simply the best.

Finally, a word to my mom and dad, whose personal experiences with work and retirement I have included in this book. I have always had the benefit of their unconditional love, the examples of their own hard work, and the inspiration of their many accomplishments to guide me. Thanks for letting me grow my own way.

Get Your Exit Strategy Ready

N THE FIRST school day of the year my father retired from teaching, he played golf. It was his way of letting the world know that he would be calling the shots, so to speak, from then on. Did he worry about paying his mortgage? How to allocate his investment assets? Whether to name **CONTINGENT BENEFICIARIES**? Nope. A check representing 75 percent of what he had earned in his last year of teaching was scheduled to arrive on the last day of the month—and every month thereafter for the rest of his life. After his death, my mom can expect to receive a check until she passes away. Plus, my dad's twenty-five years as an officer in the U.S. Air Force Reserves qualifies him to receive 50 percent of the pay he earned as a lieutenant colonel. Even I, no wizard in math, could figure out that mom and dad were going to be okay.

Dad, of course, is part of a generation that looked

to its employers to provide income for retirement. And within the ranks of old-line American companies, public school systems, and government and municipal agencies, there are still people like my dad. But their numbers have gotten smaller over the past twenty years as hundreds of new companies and small businesses have entered the marketplace and job mobility has become the norm. Even the public sector has begun to shift more of the savings burden to its employees.

Since the 1980s, most new companies have bypassed traditional retirement pension plans in favor of a new kind of retirement plan, one that requires employees to put in their own money and reduces the employer's ante to a modest matching contribution—and even that is often not required. (Many old-line companies have added these new savings plans alongside their traditional pension plans.) **DEFINED CONTRIBUTION PLANS**—that's what they're called—are cheaper for employers and a better fit with today's transient workforce. The most popular is the 401(k), which covers more than 42 million American workers. Nonprofits, hospitals, and educational institutions offer 401(k) equivalents known as 403(b)s. The government sector's version of a 401(k) is called a 457 plan. Entrepreneurs and small businesses can get in the act with SIMPLE IRAs or SIMPLE 401(k)s, SEP IRAs, and Keogh plans, plus some new offerings such as the Safe Harbor 401(k). In addition to, or instead of, a workplace retirement savings plan, something on the order of 25 percent of today's workers also have an IRA—an Individual Retirement Account.

These are the savings plans that are going to foot the bill for retirement for most twenty-first-century workers. That will come as no surprise if you are counting down to your own retirement. But you may be shocked at how many choices you have to make, how many rules and regulations you have to understand, and how many ways there are to go wrong with this money you've been nurturing so carefully during your working years. For example, do you know

◆ How much money you are going to need each month from your retirement savings to meet your budgetary requirements? Have you thought about how your financial needs will change as you age and move through the three stages of retirement?

◆ How long your money will last? How much do your investments have to earn, or "return"? What you will do if the markets turn south, as they did from 2000 through 2002, and stay there for an extended period of time?

◆ That you need to plan carefully if you want to make it easy and convenient to get at your money every month?

◆ That the rules about naming beneficiaries have changed? Have you brought your beneficiaries up to date under the **NEW IRS RULES**?

◆ How each of your retirement savings accounts will be taxed? How to avoid paying too much tax? That company stock in your retirement plan is entitled to special tax treatment?

◆ That you could be in danger of incurring a huge penalty if you make a mistake in your pattern of retirement account withdrawals? And if you do goof, you must be prepared to negotiate penalties with the IRS?

◆ When you are required to begin taking minimum withdrawals from your retirement accounts? How you can avoid taking minimum withdrawals from some accounts? And which accounts offer no flexibility?

◆ Whether you are better off accelerating withdrawals— or taking only the minimum required? (Hint: the answer depends on your financial situation and your estate planning goals.)

◆ That you could become ineligible to convert your retirement savings to a Roth IRA if you wait until you begin required withdrawals? Do you know how to manage your eligibility so that you can make a **CONVERSION** even if your salary is too high?

◆ That an IRA **ROLLOVER** is the last stop for most retirement savings—and why?

Before you throw up your hands in despair, read on. This compact, solution-saturated book will give you answers for these and dozens of other special situations. You need to know the answers to only *your* questions and the terminology that applies to only *your* choices. I've highlighted the major terms along the way and included essential information in boxes within the numbered sections. You need only enough knowledge and understanding to steer your retirement in the right direction without being overwhelmed by technical details you *don't* need to know. You won't have to become an expert in retirement tax law or IRS rules. Use our detailed table of contents to scan for topics you need to know about, or consult the index or glossary at the back of the book to help understand terminology and pinpoint answers to your own specific questions. Each glossary word will appear in bold, capitalized type the first time it appears in each of the twenty-five numbered topic discussions and here in the introduction for your convenience.

It is important to be able to see the big picture—and to have access to information about the fine points if and when the need arises. After all, you wouldn't board a plane for an exotic foreign land without understanding enough basic geography or vocabulary to find your way. You don't want to set out for retirement without a notion of the special rules, regulations, and language that describes and defines it.

But what does that mean?

While there are hundreds of subtle nuances to the rules that govern retirement savings, I believe there are twenty-five major things that you must know before you take your first dollar of retirement income. This advice will cover situations that the vast majority of earners will face. That's what this book is about. It was written to offer practical information that any reader can understand about the process of taking money out of retirement savings plans and turning it into income. You don't need to read every word of it, but you do need to zero in on the parts that apply to you. That should be easy, because the table of contents clearly spells out the topic of each section and the index can help you find those technical details you care about, such as key points about all major types of retirement plans.

One of the best things about retiring in the twenty-first century is that your job just got easier, thanks to a much-needed overhaul to the system that governs withdrawals from tax-advantaged plans and accounts. Early in 2001, the IRS issued a new set of rules and regulations that will govern retirement plan withdrawals after 2002—and other key issues associated with the process of taking money out of retirement accounts and passing them on to beneficiaries. The new rules simplified and streamlined procedures and eliminated some of the most complicated requirements.

Now, the IRS isn't generally known for making things simpler for taxpayers. So why the change of heart? I'd like to think it was because the bureaucrats finally came to their senses and said, "No one can figure this stuff out—not even the accountants and financial planners. Something has to change!" What we do know is that the number of requests for private letter rulings (from people with big bucks at stake asking for a reprieve because someone in the family screwed up or got bad advice) finally got their attention. And my guess is that the IRS looked ahead and said, "Wow! If people are confused now, what is it going to be like when 75 million baby boomers start inheriting large account balances from their parents—which is already happening—and begin taking money out of their own accounts?" It was not a pretty picture.

In my opinion, there was another motive: Taxes due on **TAX-DEFERRED** retirement savings figure to be one of the single largest sources of government revenue for the twenty-first century. Think about it: more than 4 *trillion* dollars in retirement savings waiting to be passed down to baby boomers by their parents and not a penny of it has been taxed. What's more, the IRS realized that it really had no efficient way of keeping track of what it was owed and when taxes were due.

The new rules have taken an important first step to end this madness by shifting reporting accountability to the investment companies.

Beginning in 2004, IRA custodians will have to report to account owners and the IRS on accounts that are subject to take required withdrawals. Eventually, the IRS wants to be able to check that retirees and their beneficiaries are withdrawing what they should on time and paying all the tax they owe.

But don't let all this good news about simplicity obscure the ongoing challenges of turning your retirement savings into income. The recent turmoil in the financial markets strikes a more sobering note with anyone who was counting on a robust investment climate for future security. For nearly a decade the stock market delivered positive returns. For five years running, it delivered stunning, double-digit returns. Advocates of diversification were hissed and booed as new-economy prophets proclaimed it was different this time.

Well, it wasn't. Economic expansions always end. Financial markets have always been volatile. We have had the good fortune of living through one of the strongest decades in U.S. financial history. If you're going to manage your retirement income through good *and* bad environments, you need to have information and strategies that allow for all possible scenarios.

You'll find all that and more in *Cracking Your Retirement Nest Egg*.

Understanding the Basics

Cast Your Retirement Savings into the Right Role

Decide whether your primary goal is to generate income from your retirement savings or to preserve as much of its value as you can for the next generation.

WHEN I WAS A FRESHMAN in college, I discovered that the university infirmary was well prepared for the unique afflictions of college life. After checking in at the main desk, I was told to choose one of two paths, each identified by a colored line—yellow, if I thought I had an illness such as the flu or mononucleosis, or blue, if I thought I had an injury such as a sprain or a broken bone. There was a little couch you could retreat to if you didn't fall into either category—but sure enough, most students found the right care by following yellow or blue.

The starting point for planning an approach to your retirement savings is not so different from the infirmary of my college days. Most of us fall into one of two camps: Either you need your retirement savings for income or you don't, in which case your primary goal will be to pass it on to the next generation.

It's important to identify yourself with one goal or the other before you do anything at all with your retirement savings, because the choice you make will affect dozens of your decisions. Those paths dictate where your accounts should be, how many you will need, whether to **ROLL OVER** your savings, how to handle any company stock you own, when to take your first withdrawal, how much you should take once you are required to begin withdrawing, and if a **CONVERSION** to a Roth IRA makes sense.

If you launch into retirement without one of these two goals in mind, you could stumble onto the right strategy, but who wants to leave that to chance?

This point is not obvious from everything you hear or read. Let me give you two examples. (For now, try to overlook any unfamiliar terminology. You'll master it as you go.)

At age 65, Charlie and Doreen have $200,000 in retirement savings between them. Doreen expects to receive a $40,000-a-year pension from the large consumer products company at which she has logged thirty-five years of service—70 percent of her working pay. If she dies first, Charlie will continue to receive $30,000 a year for his lifetime. Charlie, who left the workforce at 62 to pursue his interest in painting, has only his Social Security, which he has delayed until 65. That, plus Doreen's Social Security, will add another $14,000 to their annual income. They want to generate enough supplemental income from their $200,000 retirement savings—a combination of IRAs, a 403(b), and a 401(k)—to live comfortably for the rest of their lives. Their situation dictates a relatively conservative investment strategy and a relatively aggressive withdrawal strategy. Because income is their primary goal, they won't have to worry about meeting the IRS requirements to take minimum withdrawals from their savings after age 70½, because they really need the money to close the gap in their budget. Each has named the other as the primary **BENEFICIARY**, because whoever survives will need the income stream to continue to pay the bills. They have named their children as **CONTINGENT BENEFICIARIES**. That way, if something happens to both of them, their children will inherit whatever is left of their savings.

Compare their situation to that of Jeanne and Tim, who have also put away $200,000 in retirement savings, using 403(b) accounts. However, with their expected pensions as retired teachers, they can look forward to more than $90,000 a year in retirement without touching their own $200,000—and that $90,000 will increase with inflation over time. For Jeanne and Tim, the thought of turning their $200,000 savings into a nest egg for their children and a gift to their alma mater is a dream come true, especially when they consider the difference it could make to let their savings continue to grow and continue to benefit from its tax advantages. Because they have no short-term need for their savings, they can afford a relatively aggressive investment strategy and are looking for every way possible to avoid taking income. One option is to keep the minimum withdrawals that the IRS will require them to take after age 70½ to an absolute minimum. Another possibility would be to roll their savings over to an IRA then convert it to a Roth IRA. With a Roth IRA, they can avoid taking any money out of the account during their lifetimes. And when their heirs take the money, it will be 100 percent federal income tax free. There are even ways to make a gift with some of their savings that could generate a tax break and provide income if they need something more to offset possible higher health care costs in their later years. Because neither really sees the need for the money, Jeanne and Tim have named much younger beneficiaries—one more way to beat the tax man.

BEFORE YOU READ ON, take time to determine the role you have in mind for your retirement savings. Be realistic. It may seem noble to think about an inheritance for your children, but if you need your retirement savings for income, you'll end up falling short if you focus your decisions on achieving an unrealistic goal. Besides, stuff happens along the way. In the course of executing a prudent income strategy, your savings could continue to grow and you could end up with money to pass on to your heirs. In the course of executing a solid wealth-preservation strategy, you could end up with additional income, which you might put to work with charitable gifts or a life-insurance strategy that could add even more to the wealth of your heirs. But, for now, think of your retirement choices as yellow and blue lines—and pick one.

Know the Facts about Your Pension and Retirement Savings Plans

It's easier to maximize your income, lower your taxes, and avoid penalties if you understand your pension and retirement savings plans.

IF YOU PARTICIPATE in a retirement savings plan at your place of employment, if your employer offers a pension plan that will pay you income after you retire, or if you save for retirement on your own through a tax-advantaged individual retirement savings account, you have Congress to thank. Our system has gotten better and better in the years since it dawned on the collective national consciousness that we were all living longer and needed a way to pay for it. Current laws, which have been a work in progress since the 1930s, make it attractive to both employers and workers to do their part for retirement. These rules require that benefits be offered with a sense of fairness, and provide a mantle of protection to ensure that money set aside for retirement will be there when it is needed, even if an employer falls on hard times.

According to the Employee Benefit Research Institute, the first American retirement plan was established in 1759 to benefit widows and children of Presbyterian ministers. But the notion that an employer had some responsibility to look out for the later years of its loyal employees didn't really begin to catch on for another 150 years. It was consistent with the changes that were reshaping our nation from an agrarian society to an industrial one, and from rural to urban and suburban.

But the early private pension system was both inequitable and inadequate. Social Security, which wrote its first check in 1937, offered only a partial fix. A presidential commission was appointed in the early 1960s to study the system and recommend changes. In 1974, Congress passed landmark legislation that was designed to increase the number of workers who were covered by private retirement plans and to protect their benefits regardless of the fate of their employers. Employers were offered tax incentives to offer generous pension benefits, but they were also required to adhere to a strict and comprehensive set of rules and regulations, disclosures, and reporting standards. Any plan that complied with these requirements became known as a **QUALIFIED PLAN**, thus named because it qualified for special treatment under section 401 of the tax code and is governed by the Employment Retirement Income Security Act of 1974.

Today, most private sector workplace savings plans and traditional pension plans are qualified plans. Some state and local government plans, church plans, and plans for the self-employed are close enough to be considered *nearly* qualified plans. Plans that are designed primarily to benefit a select group of highly compensated individuals are **NONQUALIFIED PLANS**, generally because they fail to meet the rigorous fairness tests of qualified plans.

Does it matter whether your retirement savings are in one kind of plan or another? It does, and more important, it pays to know some basic facts about the savings and pension plans that will become your future retirement income resources. Take a few minutes to find your particular plans among the ones outlined in the pages that follow. You may need some help from your benefits or human resources office because companies are inclined to brand their plans in some corporate way rather than use the technical terms associated with them. Your employer may give an umbrella name to a package of plans and call it the Excellent Company Retirement Savings Plan. You'll have to dig deeper to find out that there are a **CASH BALANCE PENSION PLAN**, a 401(k), and

a **PROFIT SHARING PLAN** under the umbrella—all of
which you are eligible to participate in.

TODAY, MOST RETIREMENT PLANS ARE QUALIFIED PLANS

THE MAJORITY OF workplace retirement assets are in qualified plans.

Traditional pension plans and 401(k) plans (defined
more completely on page 21) are the two most common
qualified plans. Together, they account for more than
two-thirds of all retirement money outside of Social
Security.

Qualified plans offer special protections that can make
a difference both while you are saving and when you begin
taking your money out in retirement.

◆ **Traditional pensions are insured.** First, your pension benefits are protected against your employer's financial diffi-
culties. Even if your employer goes bankrupt, your pension
is insured by the Pension Benefit Guaranty Corporation
(PBGC). Your employer is required to pay annual premiums to purchase insurance for the benefits it has promised. Your individual pension benefit is guaranteed up to
$3,579 a month, an amount that is adjusted upward for
inflation.

In 2002, individual pension benefits were guaranteed
up to $3,579 a month for someone age 65. (That amount
is reduced actuarially if you are under age 65 and raised
actuarially if you are older than age 65.) If your employer's plan has sufficient assets, it is possible to receive
an amount that is even higher than the maximum guaranteed benefit.

According to the PBGC, on average, participants receive
over 90 percent of the benefits they have earned as of the
date of their plan's termination. However, some people
are cut back substantially because they stop earning benefits in the pension plan much earlier than they had
expected. As a result, hourly workers often lose the ability
to satisfy future contingencies or to receive future accru-

als, which would have resulted in a higher payout. And salaried workers don't get the benefit of final pay multipliers, which can significantly add to the pension of an individual who remains on the job for many years.

Fewer than 500 plans ended up in the hands of the PBGC during the five-year period from 1989 to 1995, according to the last comprehensive statistics compiled by the Employee Benefit Research Institute. The number tends to fall in good economic times and rise in weaker economic times. To the surprise of no one, 2002 was a record year with some high-profile bankruptcies. According to Steven Kandarian, the director of the PBGC, approximately 180,000 new participants came in under PBGC in 2002, double the previous record, which was set in 2001.

◆ **Other qualified plans are protected, too.** PBGC is the bailout for qualified pension plans. But the assets of qualified plans that are defined in terms of what *you* contribute during your working years, such as 401(k)s, profit sharing plans, **EMPLOYEE STOCK OWNERSHIP PLANS (ESOPS)**, and others, are also protected. They are held in a trust that is administered by an independent custodian. That way, no matter what happens to your employer, your savings are protected. Your employer isn't allowed to siphon funds to stave off bankruptcy, and your creditors can't get at your savings in a qualified plan. That protection is not afforded to nonqualified plans—not even to individual retirement savings accounts. Some state laws protect IRAs, but it is not clear that those laws stand up when you need them to: They've been challenged by at least one Supreme Court ruling, which held that federal law preempts all such state statutes.

Money that flows into nonqualified executive compensation plans is also vulnerable to the claims of creditors—both the firm's and the individual's. If an employer goes belly-up, as Polaroid did in 2001, the potential tax savings that many of these plans were intended to provide, along with the deferred compensation, disappears.

And, if you personally go bankrupt, you can bet that your creditors will find their way to your nonqualified plan assets without delay.

There are some additional advantages to qualified plans. They are more flexible when it comes to taking your money out. You can borrow up to $50,000 from a 401(k), for example, depending on the size of your savings (if your balance is relatively small, your limit might be $10,000). But you can't borrow from an IRA. You can make early withdrawals from your 401(k) without penalty if you encounter hardship, but not from your 403(b), which is one of those nearly qualified plans. You even have the option of special tax treatment if you conform to the rigorous rules for taking all of the money out of a qualified plan at once—an option that is not available with any other type of retirement savings plan.

TRADITIONAL DEFINED BENEFIT PENSION PLANS

TRADITIONAL PENSION PLANS are known as **DEFINED BENEFIT PLANS** because workers know from day one what they can expect to collect in terms of retirement income. That doesn't mean they know the exact dollar amount, but they do know the formula that will be used to calculate it: the "benefit" is "defined." In the private sector, a company typically funds its plan with its own money and employees are neither required nor allowed to contribute. The formula used to determine the amount of monthly income each worker will receive in retirement is usually based on some combination of years of service and income during the last (and presumably highest-paid) years of employment.

The average worker can often take home between 50 percent and 80 percent of his or her preretirement income in a monthly income stream from a traditional pension plan, but it means staying on the job for twenty years or more to qualify. In recent years, many firms have begun to offer workers an alternative to a lifetime pension called a **LUMP SUM DISTRIBUTION**: It's an amount of money that is estimated to have the potential to generate a stream of income that would be the equivalent of a monthly pension. It is based on a formula using the current yield on the 30-year U.S. Treasury bond. (More about this in Number 6.)

If you believe what you hear and read about traditional pension plans, you may think that most companies have thrown them out in favor of these alternative plans, which require employees to foot more of the bill for retirement. That's not so. Most big, established companies continue to offer traditional pension plans. But fewer people today stay on the job long enough to collect enough in traditional pension income to retire on.

It is true that few newer companies offer traditional pension plans. As new companies have grown up to become established companies in the twenty-plus years since the introduction of the 401(k),the percentage of workers employed by companies that offer traditional pension plans has dropped. But it's not because the companies gave the plans up. They didn't offer them when they were small, fledgling companies, and that didn't change when they became the new generation of big, established companies.

In the past decade, some old-line companies have also come up with hybrid versions of the traditional defined benefit pension plan in order to offer workers something that approximates the old-fashioned security of the guaranteed monthly income with a gesture toward higher job mobility. For example:

◆ **Target benefit plans** use a formula to estimate the amount the companies need to contribute in order to achieve a certain level of income for a worker, making certain assumptions about rates of return, life expectancy, and so on. The estimate is made in the worker's first year on the job, and there is no adjustment made at a later date, even if the account appears to be off target in either direction. In other words, the participant in a target benefit plan could receive the targeted amount of income, or something much higher or lower. It's just *too bad* for the worker if it is lower.

◆ **Cash balance plans** combine one of the best features of a 401(k)—its portability—with the best feature of a traditional defined benefit plan—its guaranteed benefit. Employers create individual accounts for each employee, credit them each year with a dollar amount based on a formula that may be similar to a traditional pension plan formula, and project out account values at retirement. Employees who leave after they are **VESTED** are entitled to a payout from the cash balance plan that can be taken with them or rolled over to a new employer's plan. **PENSION EQUITY PLANS** and **FLOOR PLANS** are variations on the hybrid theme.

The bad news, judging from some of the litigation that has come out of employee groups over the past five years, is that some companies have used hybrid plans—especially cash balance plans, which now account for one out of five large-company plans—to decrease their future pension burden at the expense of long-time loyal employees, who won't get the big boost in benefit accrual at the end of their working years that is typical of more traditional pension plans.

MODERN DEFINED CONTRIBUTION PLANS

CONSIDER YOURSELF FORTUNATE if you are in line to collect retirement benefits from a traditional defined benefit plan. An estimated 80 percent of the next generation of American workers will depend on plans in which a big portion of their savings came out of their own pockets. **DEFINED CONTRIBUTION PLANS** are different from defined benefit plans in precisely the way you would expect them to be: Instead of targeting the amount workers can expect to receive at the end of their working years, a defined contribution plan "defines" how much workers and employers can "contribute" each working year, based on limits set by Congress. Limits typically rise with inflation, and in 2000 the upper limits got a real boost from new legislation that added a catch-up provision for workers age 50 and over.

Many defined contribution plans are also qualified plans and as such offer the same benefit protections that apply to traditional pension plans.

◆ **Most 401(k) plans** require employees to ante up their own money for retirement savings. Money comes out of their paychecks before taxes are figured, taxes are deferred on earnings that accumulate over the years, and most enlightened employers will match employee contributions up to a certain percentage of the worker's wages. The most common match is about 3 percent. Some companies give employees a choice of how to invest their matching contributions. Others offer the match only in employer stock. Because 401(k) assets are held in trust and administered by an independent custodian, they aren't vulnerable to bankruptcy proceedings against the employer. Individual accounts are also protected against suits by your personal creditors.

◆ **Profit sharing plans** shift the burden to the employer, which makes a contribution ranging from zero to 25 percent of an individual employee's annual wages (up to $200,000, an amount that moves higher over time with inflation) to a tax-deferred savings account. There's nothing to bind an employer to an annual contribution or to a certain level of contribution. Contributions can be made even if the company isn't profitable, and the employer doesn't even have to be a for-profit organization to offer a profit sharing plan.

◆ **A money purchase plan** is similar to a profit sharing plan. However, the employer's contributions are mandatory and the amount of annual contributions is fixed. Now that the contribution limits for profit sharing plans have been raised to 25 percent, money purchase plans have lost some of their appeal.

A stock bonus plan is another variation of the profit sharing plan. Stock bonus plans require that contributions be accumulated in company stock and paid out the same way, in the form of company stock.

◆ **An employee stock ownership plan or ESOP** is a type of stock bonus plan. Employee accounts are funded with employer stock, but benefits can be paid out in cash or stock as long as the employee is free to choose payment in stock.

SMALL BUSINESS GETS INTO THE ACT

AS EARLY AS THE 1960s, Congress recognized that employees of small business and individuals who were self-employed also needed a way to save for retirement. Keogh plans were the first attempt in that direction. A Keogh plan is a qualified plan that is a lot like other corporate retirement plans. If it takes the form of a profit sharing or money purchase plan, it looks a little like a 401(k). If it takes the form of a defined benefit plan, it looks like a traditional pension plan. The idea is the same: The business owner puts away a certain amount of money for retirement, up to $40,000 a year in 2003, a total that will rise with inflation down the road. Contributions are **TAX DEDUCTIBLE**, earnings grow **TAX DEFERRED**, and withdrawals are governed by the same rules and requirements that apply to other qualified plans.

But Keoghs can also be a headache of paperwork. As a result, many small businesses were pleased when Congress in 1978 introduced an alternative in the form of a simplified employee pension individual retirement account or SEP IRA. Rules about contributions are more flexible than for some types of Keogh plans. Contribution limits are the same now; they used to be lower. And there's practically no paperwork, only one simple form to be completed at tax time. A SEP IRA is not a qualified plan. It is governed by the same rules that apply to other IRAs.

So why wouldn't any small business prefer a SEP IRA over a Keogh? There is one hitch: Employers are required to cover virtually all employees who have been on the payroll for three years. You can't do for yourself and not for those who contribute to your success. And because employees are 100 percent vested immediately, there is no way to use the retirement contribution as a reward for employees who have signed on for the long haul. By comparison, a Keogh, because it is a qualified plan, can stretch the full vesting period out for as long as six years.

In 1996, Congress addressed the limitations and weaknesses inherent in the Keogh and SEP IRA for businesses that employ fewer than 100 people but are more than just a sole proprietorship or professional practice. They introduced the Savings Incentive Match Plan for Employees, the SIMPLE 401(k) and the SIMPLE IRA. These plans promised less paperwork—and therefore less costly administration—but had lower contribution limits than their corporate counterparts. SIMPLEs got a real boost thanks to recent legislation that raised contribution limits to $8,000 in 2003 and $10,000 in 2005, and after that dictated increases in increments of $500 to keep up with inflation.

A catch-up feature allows for an additional $1,000 contribution in 2003 for workers age 50 and over, an amount that rises to $2,500 in 2006 and is scheduled to rise with inflation.

The limits are still lower than for 401(k)s and other similar defined contribution plans. But these plans have one offsetting feature: Employers are required to contribute from 1 percent to 3 percent, and depending on the percentage they choose, may have to contribute regardless of whether an employee makes a contribution.

NEARLY QUALIFIED PLANS

BECAUSE THEY PREDATE legislation that defined qualified plans, 403(b), 457, qualified annuity, and **TAX-DEFERRED ANNUITY (TDA)** plans aren't qualified plans—but they must comply with most of the same rules that apply to qualified plans. In fact, the rules that govern these plans can be more complex, but there is also some flexibility that you won't find in a qualified plan. (More about both in Number 6.)

TDAs and 403(b)s allow workers in schools and universities, hospitals, and nonprofit organizations who don't have access to the type of traditional defined benefit pension plan offered to private sector workers to save for retirement with tax-advantaged dollars. 403(b)s and 457 plans are a lot like 401(k)s in that they offer participants a variety of investment options in the form of mutual funds and the flexibility to move money from one investment to another from time to time. Money put away in a TDA is used to purchase an **INCOME ANNUITY** from an insurance company for the individual worker. Upon retirement, benefits are usually paid as a monthly annuity. However, as other retirement plans have become more flexible, other **DISTRIBUTION** options have been added. (Qualified annuity plans are sometimes used by small businesses in lieu of traditional pension plans. Contributions are used to purchase annuities for employees, which simplifies administration because there's no need for assets to be held in trust by a custodian.)

Recently, the direction has been to standardize even more of the benefits and features of 401(k), 403(b), and 457 plans. For example, beginning in 2002, the contribution limits for all three became the same, as did the new catch-up provisions. That provided a big boost for 403(b) and 457 plan participants whose contributions had been capped with lower limits until 2002.

Of all the nearly qualified plans, those that cover church workers remain among the least scrutinized. This special class of 403(b) plan was designed to offer more flexibility to religious organizations than is generally accorded to other employers. For example, a church doesn't have to cover all its employees. It can take direct charge of employee contributions, hire its own investment managers, and manage the money itself. There's even a wide degree of latitude as to what constitutes a "church." If you're covered by a church plan, it's really important to check out how it is run and what happens to your money. Some religious organizations—church-run hospitals, for example—

operate with the same high level of accountability and administrative oversight as you would find with any other employer. But many plans do not. For your own protection, you should find out.

NONQUALIFIED PLANS

COMPANIES OFTEN REWARD their top executives with the offer to set aside income in a special account to be tapped—and taxed—at retirement. Because executive deferred compensation plans lack the protections of qualified plans, they can be dicey. They may take the form of a deferred cash bonus, company stock, or stock options— and all carry their own special risks. If your employer's stock performance is disappointing, you could end up with less than you had counted on. If your employer's fiscal situation declines during the years before you collect your deferred pay, you could lose everything. The upside, of course, is nearly unlimited. Wouldn't you like to have been granted deferred compensation from Microsoft back in the mid 1980s?

INDIVIDUAL RETIREMENT ACCOUNTS

RETIREMENT PENSION AND savings plans cover groups of individuals, and they may be qualified, nearly qualified, or nonqualified. Individual retirement accounts are yet another category for retirement savings—different because they are owned and managed from beginning to end by the individual. Even SEP IRAs, which are cited above as options for small business, are really accounts, not plans, although they must be initiated by a business owner on behalf of the employee. With all other individual retirement accounts, you are truly on your own. You decide whether to contribute to them, whether to consolidate or **TRANSFER** assets among them, and how to manage them.

◆ **Traditional IRAs** offer tax-deductibility to a relatively small group of workers who don't have access to a retirement plan at work or who earn less than $34,000 ($54,000 for married couples). If you earn between $34,000 and

HIGHER LIMITS FOR RETIREMENT SAVINGS PLANS

TYPE OF ACCOUNT	NEW CONTRIBUTION LIMITS	BEGINNING	SAVERS AGE 50+ CAN ADD AN EXTRA	BEGINNING
IRAs	$3,000	in 2002	$500	in 2002
	$4,000	in 2005		
			$1,000	in 2006
	$5,000	in 2008[1]		
401(k), 403(b), 457	$11,000	in 2002	$1,000	in 2002
	$12,000	in 2003	$2,000	in 2003
	$13,000	in 2004	$3,000	in 2004
	$14,000	in 2005	$4,000	in 2005
	$15,000	in 2006[2]	$5,000	in 2006
SIMPLE IRA	$7,000	in 2002	$500	in 2002
	$8,000	in 2003	$1,000	in 2003
	$9,000	in 2004	$1,500	in 2004
	$10,000	in 2005[2]	$2,000	in 2005
			$2,500	in 2006[3]
SEP IRA	In 2002: Up to 25% of the first $200,000 you earn up to $40,000			
Keogh	In 2002: Up to 25% of the first $200,000 you earn up to $40,000			

[1] After 2008, increases adjusted for inflation in $500 increments
[2] After 2006, increases adjusted for inflation in $500 increments
[3] Assumes no inflation adjustment for 2006

SOURCE: INTERNAL REVENUE SERVICE

$44,000 ($54,000 and $64,000 for married couples), you're entitled to a partial deduction.

But you can contribute to a traditional IRA even if you can't take the tax deduction, and if you have already maxed out your workplace retirement savings contributions, you should indeed take advantage of your ability to contribute to an IRA for yourself and your spouse, even if only one of you is employed. Beginning in 2002, you can contribute $3,000 each year to an IRA, an amount that

rises to $5,000 in 2008 and continues to rise in $500 increments to offset the impact of inflation. Wage earners who
are age 50 and over can also make catch-up contributions
of $500, an amount that rises to $1,000. However, there is
no provision for this $1,000 catch-up amount to increase
for inflation.

◆ **Contribution limits for Roth IRAs** are the same as for traditional IRAs, but there are eligibility requirements associated with Roth IRAs. You can't earn more than $110,000
if you're single (or $160,000 if you're married and filing
jointly) and contribute to a Roth IRA. Your contributions
to a Roth IRA are never tax deductible, but there's a tan-
talizing alternative benefit: If you have your account for at
least five years and keep your hands off the earnings until
you are 59½, all of your withdrawals are tax free. For more
about Roth IRA withdrawals, see Number 18.

◆ **Rollover IRAs** aren't really contributory accounts, so they
don't really belong in this list of plans and accounts. However, you're going to hear a lot more about them later in
the book. For years, no one paid much attention to rollover IRAs. They were designed as facilitators, to help
workers move money out of a workplace savings plan without giving up the mantle of tax deferral. The astounding
truth is that, sooner or later, most of your tax-advantaged
savings are likely to end up in a rollover IRA. So I'll tell you
what you need to know about them as we go along.

Get the Essentials in Order

When to Get Started—and How

Give yourself two to five years to put your investment strategy in place, six months to one year to get paperwork in order.

FOR MOST AMERICANS, retirement is a goal that is dreamed about, planned for, and marked on calendars well in advance. Your employer may enforce a mandatory retirement at a certain age, or you may have a date fixed in your own mind for your departure from the working world. Assuming that the timing for your retirement is in your hands (you hope it won't be sprung on you without notice), ideally you should give yourself at least five years to get your finances, investments, and income strategy in order—along with all the paperwork that comes with the territory. (There are a lot of other things to consider—health care, life insurance, long-term care—all matters for other books.) If that sounds like a long time, consider that investment strategies need attention well in advance, so that you don't find yourself at the mercy of the stock and bond markets. Some employers—typically small companies—can take up to a year to release your retirement savings. Rollovers and other account action can also take six months to a year.

THE FIVE-YEAR COUNTDOWN

THERE'S SOMETHING A little chicken-and-eggish about the five-year countdown to retirement. First you have to have a retirement date in mind. Then you have to make sure you have enough saved to retire on that date. If the calculations are not working out, you have to go back and adjust the date. And so on. If you're diligent, it's a good idea to have a target in mind five, ten, or even twenty years in advance, and to check your progress from time to time to make sure you're still on track.

FIVE YEARS BEFORE YOUR INTENDED RETIREMENT DATE, REVIEW YOUR INVESTMENT STRATEGY

THE DEBATE OVER retirement investment strategies is likely to go on forever. Most financial experts advise you to start the process of becoming more conservative with your investments as early as ten years before you retire. Yet plenty of studies show that you should keep a fairly aggressive mix of investments all the way through retirement—bracing yourself for periods of volatility—and not losing faith when they occur. Determining which camp you fall into is personal. If you're an experienced investor, you may feel well equipped to make any adjustments to your strategy on your own. If you're feeling like you could use some professional advice, now's the time. With a five-year start, you can take advantage of the market's natural volatility to sell into strength and buy into weakness. (More on investment strategy in Number 15.) Generally speaking, the more likely you are to need your retirement savings to generate income that will pay the bills, the less risk you should take with your assets. The less likely you are to need your retirement savings to cover your monthly income needs, the more risk you can afford to take. Life's like that.

If you own company stock in an **EMPLOYEE STOCK OWNERSHIP PLAN (ESOP)**, you have a five-year window before retirement in which you can begin to liquidate your position, penalty free. There are important tax considerations that apply to company stock. You need to look at your entire financial picture before you take any steps to take possession of your shares or sell your position, but it is good to know that you have the right to take some action on the stock during this five-year period. You are probably in a better position than anyone else—even most investment professionals—to assess your employer's financial health going forward. But that's no guarantee that you won't be hit with an unpleasant revelation. Employees at Enron, the Houston-based energy company that declared bankruptcy in 2001, probably expected a rosy future for their firm right up until the last months. But employees at Polaroid, which suffered the same fate, should have seen the writing on the wall. After the stock price hit a high of about $60 a share in mid-1997, employees who were savvy enough to know about this five-year window sold their stock. Those who didn't watched the stock fall to less than $1 a share before the company declared bankruptcy in 2001.

TWO YEARS BEFORE YOUR TARGETED RETIREMENT DATE, ASSESS YOUR FINANCIAL RESOURCES AND FUTURE INCOME NEEDS

THE CONVENTIONAL WISDOM is that you will need 60 percent to 80 percent of your working income to live reasonably well in retirement. But frankly, I can't find anyone who knows the source of those ranges, and they are so broad that they are not really very useful. Deciding how much you will need for your *own* retirement requires a careful analysis of your current lifestyle and how you expect it to change during the three stages of retirement, which have been defined by a number of recent retirement studies. I like the description of early, mid-, and late-stage retirement that came out of a University of North Texas study in the early 1990s.

◆ **Early stage retirees (ages 65 to 74)** are characterized by relatively good health and unrestricted mobility. Many early stage retirees work part-time or pursue a new career path that may be hobby-related: the teacher who becomes a handyman or the office worker who takes on residential landscaping assignments. It's not uncommon for early stage retirees to need nearly 100 percent of their pre-retirement income. Wardrobe and commuting costs may go down, but most retirees want to have additional funds for travel and recreation. During these years, most retirees seek to conserve or even increase their retirement resources with an eye to living another twenty-five to thirty-five years. Decisions to accelerate or to postpone Social Security and IRA withdrawals can make a significant difference in the amount of money that will be available during later stages of retirement.

◆ **Midstage retirement (75 to 84)** finds most retirees really ready to slow down. The number of Americans who work beyond age 75 declines sharply, and that means their financial resources become fixed—and may actually begin to decline at this stage. At age 70½, you are required to start taking money out of your traditional IRAs and your workplace savings plans (unless you are still working for a company where you are not one of the head honchos). Budgets begin to change dramatically during midstage retirement. Fewer dollars are spent on home decorating, home improvements, and autos, as many retirees give up their wheels. Health care expenditures—especially for prescription drugs—tend to rise.

◆ **Late-stage retirement (85 and over)** sees spending patterns shift further as health care and home-care services increase and travel and hobbies decrease. Social Security accounts for an increasing percentage of total income for Americans in this age bracket. At this point, it's important to conserve financial resources so that you have enough predictable income to live out your years in comfort.

If you assume that you need to plan for thirty years of income after retirement, how will you know whether your current resources will allow you to retire on schedule and live comfortably? Start with what you know. Use historical standards and probabilities to project your expectations for income from your retirement savings. And don't forget to factor in inflation. Every major financial website offers a calculator to help you determine whether your retirement resources will last a lifetime. Some are far better than others. For example, the calculators at financial

engines.com and moneycentral.msn.com/retire/planner
.asp build probabilities into their projections, which means
they will tell you the level of confidence you can have in
your estimates. Given your asset mix, your savings rate, and
your withdrawal rate, plus the number of years over which
you expect to take income, these calculators can tell you
whether you are likely to reach your retirement savings
goal, if you are still in savings mode, and how likely it is
that your savings will last.

This more sophisticated approach is better than a
straight-line approach built on the assumption that your
investments will earn a certain percent a year. Even if you
work with a conservative assumption about return, it
doesn't take into consideration the ups and downs of the
market and the likely impact of market volatility on your
investments as you enter and pass through retirement.

But you can start with a ballpark approach and then
refine it as you go along. Here's what I mean: Say your
household income is $75,000 a year—before taxes—and
you want to target $60,000 a year for your first year of
retirement at age 66. You're comfortable with that same
level of income throughout retirement, but you understand that you should plan for it to rise about 3 percent to
4 percent a year to keep up with inflation.

When you assess your resources, here's what you find.
You're entitled to collect $14,000 a year in Social Security
at age 66. Your Social Security benefits are scheduled to
keep pace with inflation. You expect to receive $14,000 a
year in retirement pension income from your last
employer, also indexed for inflation. That means you'll
need to generate $32,000 in the first year of retirement to
bridge the gap between what you need and what you know
you will receive. And you need a plan to increase your
income to keep up with inflation.

Now, shift your thinking, for a moment, to how much
money you will need to accumulate to generate $32,000 a
year plus for the next thirty years. The figure is probably a
lot larger than you expect. That's because most financial

experts believe that you should not withdraw more than 3 percent to 4 percent of your retirement nest egg each year, in order to ensure that your assets will last as long as you need them. That means you'll need something on the order of $1 million in retirement and personal savings to meet your income needs—and that your nest egg will need to continue to grow at about 6 percent to 7 percent over the long term.

And you thought $1 million would buy you the moon!

On one hand, a 3 percent to 4 percent withdrawal rate is conservative and the return estimate may seem conservative, too. But when you consider the the financial markets of 2000 through 2002, it's clear that a rough patch can take its toll, and all of us need to plan for years when the markets don't produce double-digit returns.

What can you do if your income needs seem wildly out of touch with your financial resources? Generally speaking, you'll need to reduce your expectations, adjust your investment strategy to take on more risk, or postpone retirement. And you'll need to go back to those tomes in the bookstore that talk about saving for retirement. This book is meant to pick up where they leave off. It assumes you have reached your destination, and that you have packed everything you need for this trip.

AT TWO YEARS, ALSO COMPILE PHYSICAL EVIDENCE OF ALL YOUR FINANCIAL AND RETIREMENT RESOURCES AND REVIEW YOUR INVESTMENT STRATEGY

IF YOU HAVE WORKED for multiple employers, it's a good idea to do a quick job history and review the list of retirement resources that will be at your disposal. If you have left retirement savings in the care of previous employers, you'll need to make decisions about what to do with those funds. Otherwise, your former employer may make the decision for you. Most workplace retirement savings plans require that you take your money out by age 65 or turn your savings into a **SYSTEMATIC WITHDRAWAL PLAN** that will be arranged by the investment firm that manages the plan.

At minimum, prepare a list of addresses and contacts so that you can check the status of your savings. Before you take any action, it's a good idea to contact your former employers and ask them for a report on the status of your benefits. For any **QUALIFIED PLAN** you've participated in, ask for a summary of the **PLAN DOCUMENT**. That way you can review key components, such as **DISTRIBUTION** options, that may help you put your future plans in order.

Employers are required to stay in touch with former employees who are entitled to future benefits or who have left money in retirement savings accounts. They must also make a good faith effort to find you if you have moved. But don't wait for the phone to ring. Take the first step yourself. In the past two decades, mergers, acquisitions, and name changes have made it easy for former employees to fall through the cracks. The only person who can ensure that does not happen to you is you.

Create a file listing the locations of all individual retirement accounts, personal investments and savings accounts, and certificates of deposit. Gather any physical certificates or documents, such as U.S. savings bonds, or insurance or annuity policies.

Your goal is to have physical evidence of all your financial resources in a single place as you proceed with your countdown to retirement.

The last task for this time period: Recheck the decisions you made at the five-year mark and make sure they still make sense. I can't stress the importance of reviewing your strategy at each step of the way, making sure you are still on track.

ONE YEAR BEFORE YOUR TARGETED RETIREMENT DATE, CONTACT SOCIAL SECURITY, ARRANGE FOR ROLLOVERS FROM ANY FORMER RETIREMENT SAVINGS PLANS, AND MEET WITH YOUR CURRENT EMPLOYER

IF YOU EXPECT to commence your Social Security benefits when you retire, contact your local Social Security office one year before your retirement date. Within the past calendar year, you should have received a complete history of your Social Security records and an estimate of how much you can expect to receive in benefits. Take time to verify the accuracy of that report and request a more recent one if you expect it to reflect any significant change, for example, if your spouse has passed away. (Number 14 explores Social Security in greater detail.)

Regardless of where your retirement savings have resided over your working years, now is the time to bring them together under your control. That's true whether you're going to manage them yourself or turn them over to a financial adviser. The rollover process has become more streamlined within big financial companies, but it's not unusual for a rollover to take six months when it should take six weeks. Generally speaking, the smaller and less experienced the institution you are working with— at either end—the longer the process. (We'll get to more on rollover strategies in Number 9.)

Who is the person to contact at your employer? Your human resources or benefits office should be able to answer all questions about your pension benefits and retirement savings. Today, many employers have out-sourced this function to a benefits manager, and you may find yourself dealing with an 800 number and representatives of the benefits management company. Although they should be very well prepared to answer your questions and dig up information you need, have the name and phone number of a person within your firm who can run interference if you don't feel you're getting the attention you deserve. There's nothing like having a real person on your side.

SIX MONTHS BEFORE YOUR DATE, CONSOLIDATE, DESIGNATE, AND OPEN NEW ACCOUNTS

IN THE NEXT NUMBER and in Number 16, I'll get into details about accounts and income planning. For now, what you need to know is that you may be entitled to a special tax treatment called **TEN-YEAR FORWARD AVERAGING**

FIVE-YEAR COUNTDOWN CHECKLIST

Five years
◆ Review your investment strategy

Two years
◆ Assess your financial resources and future income needs
◆ Organize documentation and records of retirement plans and accounts
◆ Review your investment strategy

One Year
◆ Contact Social Security
◆ Rollover savings, where appropriate
◆ Ask your employer to review all financial benefits

Six Months
◆ Consolidate retirement savings accounts and open new accounts for your income plan
◆ Check out eligibility for favorable tax strategies

on some portion of your retirement savings. You may be able to treat some of your retirement savings as **CAPITAL GAINS** and pay tax on it at a lower rate (most retirement withdrawals are taxed as **ORDINARY INCOME**).

Or, you may be entitled to special tax treatment on company stock you own in a qualified plan. The rules that govern all these options are complex, and the processes involved can take some time and planning. Give yourself at least six months to weigh these options and to execute them. Look for more detail in Numbers 10 and 21.

Organization, Consolidation, and Paperwork

You need a "back-office" plan to make your job easy and convenient.

IF YOU EXPECT TO FUND a large part of your retirement income from your tax-advantaged retirement savings, organization can save you time and paperwork later, make it easier to create a retirement "paycheck"—and even save you money. If you're among the fortunate people for whom retirement savings is primarily an asset you plan to pass on to the next generation (except for **REQUIRED MINIMUM DISTRIBUTIONS**—the amounts that the IRS will require you to withdraw after age 70½), your challenge is somewhat different. You may be able to delay some of the basic organizational steps that are discussed here. But don't assume that you are off the hook.

With that advice in mind, consider how different your work will be from the job of retirees who traveled this way from a previous generation: It didn't take much in the way of organization to go to the mailbox once a month for a pension and/or a Social Security check. However, with a wider variety of savings options and complex rules governing withdrawals and taxes, the likelihood of a costly error goes up if you don't have a game plan for your retirement finances. Your goal should be to reduce your efforts to a few basic steps each month plus a session at year end to take care of issues such as **REBALANCING** your portfolio, estimating taxes, and meeting other IRS requirements. In the investment business, the term "back office" is used to describe the labor-intensive grunt work that makes it possible to keep the operation going. You need a back-office organization to keep your retirement working smoothly, too. Here are five basic steps that can get you started.

IDENTIFY AND CATEGORIZE ACCOUNTS

IF YOU HAVE FOLLOWED the advice provided in Number 3 to make a list of all your retirement accounts and resources, now is the time to put it to work. Divide it into the following three categories:

◆ **Tax-advantaged workplace savings accounts**—all 401(k), 403(b), 457, and other workplace savings plans, including SEP IRAs and Keogh plans and accounts to which you made after-tax contributions, such as a company thrift plan.

◆ **Tax-advantaged individual retirement savings accounts**— your IRAs and any **TAX-DEFERRED ANNUITIES** you've purchased on your own.

◆ **Taxable savings**—your brokerage account, mutual funds, CDs, and savings bonds.

For each account, you'll want a contact name, phone number, and if it's relevant, an e-mail address. You'll also want to check on the procedure for rolling your tax-advantaged savings over into a new account, and time necessary for that process to be completed, a copy of any forms you'll need to use, and information about any restrictions that apply. For example, if you own any unusual assets, such as artwork, real estate, or **RESTRICTED STOCK**, there may be time constraints that govern your access, and you should understand what they are.

CHOOSE A FINANCIAL SUPERMARKET OR HIRE A FINANCIAL ADVISER

AS YOU STRIVE FOR an efficient income and investment process, you'll need a "Retirement Central" for your assets. If you're comfortable with managing your own account, your Retirement Central might be a **FINANCIAL SUPERMARKET** that offers access to a wide range of financial assets, an experienced rollover team, and other services that can make your life easier. In my extensive experience, there are only a handful of companies that have all these resources and can deliver them with superior service. Charles Schwab, Fidelity, Vanguard, and T. Rowe Price all qualify. Some online brokers, such as Harris-*direct,* also fit the bill.

What do these companies have in common? Each offers access to thousands of mutual funds, stocks, bonds, and other types of more complex investments. Each has a wealth of educational and informational resources, especially through their websites, which offer third-party research, sophisticated calculators and planning tools, and online news. Most will also let you customize a home page so that the news and information you value most is right there, front and center, each time you log in.

Schwab, Fidelity, Vanguard, and T. Rowe Price all do a pretty good job of handling rollover transactions, which is a much bigger deal than you might think. You may only have to go through the process once, but it's enough of a challenge that it can be a deal breaker if you find that your company is falling down on the job—or even takes much longer than it should. We surveyed a dozen financial providers and found that these four were fast, helpful, accurate, and knowledgeable about some of the tricky details that can figure into a rollover. All four have specialists trained in the rollover process.

The best thing about a financial supermarket is that you can still get access to that favorite fund that is managed by a smaller firm, a boutique, or a niche market player. Most small to midsized fund companies have **DISTRIBUTION** arrangements with a supermarket, and the modest account fee you'll pay is worth it for the convenience of having all of the information you want in one place.

Supermarkets cater to self-directed investors. If you want a hand to hold, or something more—a financial adviser or investment manager—a supermarket is probably not a good match. You could steer yourself specifically into a supermarket's asset management services, but I think that a firm that caters primarily to self-directed investors has some trouble serving clients who need more help. At many supermarket investor centers, both the attitude and the pace of the service communicate an expectation that the customer ought to know *something*, for heaven's sake.

So if you're feeling a little clueless about this nest egg that has to last a lifetime, consider a firm that will take charge of your goals and the decisions that come along with achieving them. Full service brokers, such as Merrill Lynch, who have redefined themselves as financial advisers in the past decade, target the investor who needs help. You're going to pay for the extra time and service, but that should be okay if you get what you need: A financial professional who can steer you in the right direction. Smaller firms, regional firms, even local firms that come through a recommendation, all can help you create a plan for retirement income, advise you on investment strategy, and execute it for you. Some small firms or independent financial advisers turn down accounts that are less than $1 million or handle them differently—you get a lower level of service and what I call batch-processed, or generic, investment advice. That's not necessarily bad if the advice is also solid and responsible and your affairs are uncomplicated. Look for an investment manager who is accustomed to working with clients who have assets in the same range as yours.

The most important criteria in choosing a Retirement Central for your own accounts are your comfort level and any special needs you may have, such as attention to your small business succession plan or long-term planning for a disabled child. Look for an adviser with experience that matches your special needs. A financial supermarket will eat up fewer of your investment dollars in fees and charges, but it will require that you are comfortable in the role of managing partner. A financial adviser—whether a big national firm or a small boutique—will go heavier on the service. You should expect a plan of action that is tailored to your specific needs. However, if you have never worked with a financial adviser, take time and considerable care in making your choice. A good recent book on the topic of choosing a financial adviser is *The Right Way to Hire Financial Help* by *Boston Globe* personal finance editor Charles A. Jaffee (MIT Press, 2001).

CONSOLIDATE YOUR ACCOUNTS FOR MAXIMUM EFFICIENCY

WHAT DOES YOUR account list look like? If it is anything like my friend Sam's, you have your work cut out for you. Sam started investing twenty-five years ago, when his mother left him a modest sum in savings bonds and a single bank CD. He keeps the savings bonds in a desk drawer. He has continued to **ROLL OVER** the CD at his local bank, which has been merged so many times he can't remember what it was called when he first started to do business there. His small local bank is now a major regional bank, and it also holds the CDs he has bought on his own, which range in maturity from six months to five years and are worth more than $50,000.

Sam will be eligible to collect Social Security when he turns 67, but he would like to slow down to a part-time schedule in five years, at age 55. He figures he can supplement his part-time consulting income with withdrawals from his retirement savings. In addition to his savings bonds and CDs, Sam has

◆ $100,000 in a 403(b) account at a hospital where he was an administrator in the mid-1980s

◆ $200,000 in a 401(k) at a pharmaceutical firm he worked at in the 1990s

◆ $200,000 in a SEP IRA that he accumulated during the past ten years as an independent consultant and divided between two accounts, one at Vanguard and the other at Fidelity

◆ $50,000 in traditional IRAs at Schwab. About $20,000 of the $50,000 is in a tax-deductible IRA that he opened with a $2,000 contribution in the late 1980s.

◆ $8,000 in Roth IRAs, which he decided to keep at

T. Rowe Price specifically to keep them separate from his other accounts.

◆ $5,000 in Walt Disney stock in a taxable account. He bought it when it was bargain priced. (He's still waiting for his bargain to appreciate.)

Whew!

Now, your resources may not be quite as scattered as Sam's, but if you have changed jobs five to eight times in the course of your career—a number that is not unusual these days—it may not be that far off course. And like Sam, you most likely need to rein in all these accounts and bring some order to your financial situation through consolidation.

Consolidation is essential for more than one reason: Not only will it be inconvenient to create income if you have your accounts at too many different institutions, you'll also give up valuable flexibility at tax time. (More about that in Number 11.) When it comes time to begin required minimum withdrawals from your tax-advantaged accounts, you have a lot more control over where you take your distributions under new IRS guidelines issued in 2001. Also, most employers won't let you leave your retirement savings with them indefinitely. And because company savings plans typically offer fewer options for withdrawing your money, at some point it's a good idea to consider moving all of your workplace savings into an IRA.

Once you've selected your Retirement Central, you're ready to consolidate. If you decide to work with a financial adviser, he or she will take charge of your accounts. Most independent advisers work with firms that handle account transactions and often provide **CUSTODIAL SERVICES** for the assets they manage. If you choose to work with a financial supermarket, you are in charge of the consolidation process—and it is important to have a plan laid out before you take your first step. Your goal is to

◆ bring all **TAX-DEFERRED** and taxable assets under one company's roof

◆ create as few accounts as are necessary to preserve tax benefits and flexibility

◆ follow the rules about rollovers and account **TRANSFERS** with great care to avoid paying taxes prematurely or penalties unnecessarily (see Number 11)

◆ identify any amounts that may be eligible for special tax treatment and weigh your options before you execute your consolidation plan (see Number 11)

Here's what that means for most individuals:

◆ **A rollover IRA account.** In your rollover account, you'll consolidate all tax-advantaged savings from prior employers. Remember Sam's 403(b), his 401(k), and his SEP IRA? Now that the IRS has relaxed rules on combining savings from different kinds of accounts, he can consolidate all of these savings in a single rollover IRA. (More about rollovers in Number 9.)

◆ **Separate accounts for different types of IRAs.** Continue to maintain separate accounts for deductible traditional IRAs, nondeductible traditional IRAs, and any Roth IRAs that you have. There's no rule against combining both types of traditional IRAs, but your tax situation will be more complicated if you do. You'll owe taxes on both principal and earnings of tax-deductible traditional IRAs and only on the earnings of nondeductible IRAs. If your balances in one type of traditional IRA are significantly smaller than in others, consider drawing the balance of the smaller account down faster and you'll soon have one less account to deal with.

◆ **Consolidate taxable savings under the same umbrella account that holds your tax-advantaged savings.** Money in a brokerage account and any other individual securities that are resources for retirement can be held in the same umbrella account in a financial supermarket but kept separate from your tax-advantaged savings. Even CDs and U.S. Treasury bonds can be held in your Retirement Central account. Say goodbye to your bank, Sam.

CREATE SEPARATE ACCOUNTS FOR EMERGENCIES AND SPENDING

THINKING OF YOUR RESOURCES as one big pot—a single source that provides ample money to live on and funds for emergencies while it continues to appreciate in value at the same time—takes consolidation too far. Numbers 15 and 16 provide more specific guidance on creating strategies for investment and income. For now, keep in mind that these goals are separate and as such are best handled out of separate accounts.

LEARN WHAT THE INTERNET CAN DO FOR YOU

IF YOU DECIDE THAT part of retirement is leaving computers behind—or if you don't see yourself picking up a new skill if it was never part of your work life—you will need to accept a great deal more paperwork and commit a great deal more time to managing your finances. It's your call, but I think you will find yourself truly handicapped if you decide to go into retirement in the twenty-first century without computer tools.

Even an Internet neophyte should have no problem managing retirement finances online. The number of online tools has exploded in the past five years, and most websites have been designed for easy navigation. If you take advantage of your Retirement Central's offers to provide your statements, prospectuses, reports, and other information online, you can kiss most paperwork goodbye. Many companies have even formed relationships with Intuit, the leading provider of TurboTax tax software, to make it easy to link your account information to current tax forms to help you calculate taxes on your taxable investments. And you can download information directly from your Form 1099-R, which reports retirement plan withdrawals. You won't have to enter anything manually, and many companies offer discounts on the software.

That said, some items are clearly easier to use if you get them via the U.S. mail. I have found through focus group research that while most investors are happy enough to see their account balances on the computer screen, the majority still want to receive paper copies of educational newsletters and magazines from their investment company. There's something beneficial about being able to toss them into a bag for reading at your leisure and at your own pace. Maybe that will change another generation down the road—but most people are not there yet.   .

You may also want to be sent a printed copy of each year-end report—a paper trail of transactions to refer to down the road. Even that is not essential, but it can be comforting.

KEEP PAPERWORK TO A MINIMUM

IF YOU WORK ONLINE, you will automatically limit the paper you have to deal with. And whether it's online or on paper, here's what you'll need to keep track of over time:

◆ Minimum distribution requirements after age 70½. If some of your retirement savings are on a different minimum distribution calendar than others, this requires special attention.

◆ **BENEFICIARY** forms.

◆ Paperwork documenting rollovers and **CONVERSIONS** (for up to three years).

◆ **COST BASIS** for taxable investments. Your investment company will probably calculate this for you. But there's more than one formula, and if you're a stickler for detail, you'll want to talk with a tax adviser about other options.

◆ Your portfolio **ASSET ALLOCATION**. Many investment company websites offer software that provides a current overview of your portfolio in a pie chart format, showing percentages by major asset class or investment style category. Why do you need to track asset allocation? So you can rebalance when it deviates from your goals.

◆ Records of the disposition, either by sale or gift, of company stock you took **IN KIND** from a workplace retirement plan on which you will owe **CAPITAL GAINS** tax on the **NET UNREALIZED APPRECIATION**.

◆ **MATURITY DATES** of bonds in **LADDERED** investment

IRS FORMS FOR REPORTING RETIREMENT DISTRIBUTIONS

FORM	NAME
4972	Tax on Lump-Sum Distributions
5329	Additional Taxes On Qualified Plans (including IRAs) and Other Tax-Favored Accounts
5330	Return of Excise Taxes Related to Employee Benefit Plans
8606	Nondeductible IRAs and Coverdell ESAs

portfolios, certificates of deposit (CDs), and the status of savings bonds.

◆ Special IRS forms for the reporting of retirement distributions. Different forms apply to regular distributions, early distributions—where penalties may apply—and missed distributions. (See the box above for an inventory of special forms.)

BENEFICIARY FORMS ARE best kept in paper form. You'll need several copies. They belong with your will, copies of your insurance policies, and other essential paperwork that applies to your estate. A long-range calendar can help you track items such as bond maturity dates and other key dates that require some action on your part.

What about all the paper that you receive from your investment companies? If you consolidate your accounts with a single investment provider, that cuts out reports and marketing information from multiple companies. If you hone your collection of mutual funds and financial accounts, there will be fewer reports to read. And finally, if you elect to receive statements, transaction confirmations, and other routine reporting information online, your desk should stay fairly clean. Otherwise, be sure to keep your annual statements as long as your accounts are active. You can toss out anything that is summarized in your year-end annual statement.

5

How to Choose, Change, and Keep Track of Your Beneficiaries

Your beneficiary form is the will for your retirement account. Keep it in a safe place.

WHEN YOU OPENED your first IRA or signed up for your employer's workplace retirement savings, you may not have given much thought to your **BENEFICIARIES**. If you're like most of us, you chose your spouse, your children, your parents, or some combination of family members for whom you feel affection and responsibility. And you almost certainly didn't give much thought to the beneficiary *form* you were asked to complete as part of your account paperwork. In fact, until recently, if you left that part of your application blank, no one would have called you on it.

However, as the amount of money invested in retirement savings accounts has grown, more attention is being paid to how it will be passed down and to whom, and what that means to the actual value of the accounts. Now that the rules associated with beneficiaries of retirement accounts have been overhauled by a sympathetic IRS, some aspects of choosing and changing your beneficiaries have actually gotten easier.

Under the **OLD RULES**, in effect before the IRS proposed sweeping rule changes in 2001, your choice of beneficiary could play a role in determining how rapidly you were required to take money out of your retirement savings in the years after you turned 70½. That was important because, as a general rule, thanks to tax deferral, the longer you stretch out your withdrawals, the more your account is worth. And the slower you take your money out, the lower your annual tax bill will be. Now the **NEW RULES** have given just about everyone the option to take lower minimum withdrawals, which can translate into a considerable annual tax savings. For individuals with mega-millions in their retirement savings accounts, something other than taxes may drive withdrawal decisions and slower withdrawals may not be the best strategy. But for most Americans, the ideal way to treat a retirement account is to keep it sheltered from taxes as long as possible. And that—as you will see when you read further—can be influenced by whom you name as your beneficiary.

The beneficiary you name may determine the ultimate value of your retirement savings account after you're gone—a point that is not easily grasped. You may look at your $50,000 savings and see $50,000. But depending on whom you name and what your beneficiary does when the money is inherited, it could be worth $35,000 or $1 million—no exaggeration.

Now, in some sense, that is not your problem. But if you want your heirs to make the most out of the money you've saved, it is essential to consider what the rules allow, to follow them to the letter, and to avoid any decisions that could be an obstacle to your goal.

NAMING A BENEFICIARY

YOU CAN NAME ANYONE you want as beneficiary of your retirement savings account—your cat, your cousin, or your alma mater. But if your goal is to pass on the benefits of tax deferral along with your retirement savings, it's a good idea to choose beneficiaries who qualify as **DESIGNATED BENEFICIARIES** by IRS standards. Here's what that means: You must name a person—as opposed to an institution (or your cat). You can also name a trust that has been structured to meet the following four criteria: It must be a valid trust under the laws of your state of residence. It must be an **IRREVOCABLE TRUST**—you can't change your mind about it or its terms—or it must become irrevocable upon your death. The trust's beneficiaries must be human individuals and identifiable, even though you don't need to identify them by name in the trust. In other words, you can name your "children" as beneficiaries, leaving open the possibility that you may have more—or fewer—children when the trust kicks in than you did when it was created. You must submit a list of beneficiaries of the trust, clearly indicating who gets what and any special conditions, to the custodian of your retirement savings plan or IRA. Or you can provide a copy of the trust and any subsequent amendments, but it's usually easier to pass on a list of beneficiaries. And in many cases, you can provide this information on the custodian's beneficiary form without any further fuss.

What happens if you want to name a non-person beneficiary, say a charity or an educational or religious institution? You are free to do so. Although you will have no designated beneficiary, that's not the same as having no beneficiary at all. The consequences of having a nondesignated beneficiary only come into play when the money is passed on. Because your beneficiary has no life expectancy, the money in your account will be forced out of the account more rapidly. But so what? If you've left your money to a nonprofit, it won't have to pay taxes, and the sooner it gets its hands on your money, the better.

WHOM TO CHOOSE

IT MAY SEEM OBVIOUS whom you should name as your beneficiary. If your spouse needs income after you are gone, you almost certainly will name your spouse. If you're a single parent, you want to provide for your children. If your retirement assets are more than you will ever need to live on, you may want some or all of the money to go to charity. But as obvious as these choices seem, you may not know the trade-offs or the impact your choices may have on the ultimate value of your savings. These few facts may influence your selection:

◆ **Spouses get special treatment.** Most married couples name their spouses, but did you know that spouses are the only beneficiaries who have the option of rolling over inherited retirement assets to their own names? This may or may not be a good idea (more about inherited accounts in Number 24). But it's a nice option to have. Just be sure to name your spouse as your **SOLE BENEFICIARY**—not one of multiple beneficiaries—or the option goes away.

If your spouse is ten years or more younger than you are, you're entitled to use a special table when it comes time to calculate the amount you're required to withdraw from your retirement savings accounts each year after you reach age 70½. (See Number 13.)

But if your spouse does not need access to your retirement savings, you will do well to consider another, even younger beneficiary. The additional assets may add to your spouse's own estate tax planning challenges, and the money might have more potential if left to a younger beneficiary (see below). Or you can name a younger **CONTINGENT BENEFICIARY** if your spouse's needs could go either way and you want to preserve some additional flexibility. If your spouse needs the assets, they are available. If your spouse does not need the assets, he or she can disclaim them and the younger, contingent beneficiary steps in.

◆ **Naming a younger beneficiary can make your retirement assets last longer.** After you're gone, your beneficiary's life expectancy will govern the rate at which the IRS requires withdrawals from the inherited account. And that can make an enormous difference—even in the value of a relatively small account. An example makes this easier to understand:

At 70½, you are preparing to take your first minimum withdrawal from your IRA. If your 70-year-old spouse is your sole beneficiary, he or she would continue to take withdrawals at the same rate after you passed away. However, if you named your 20-year-old grandson as your beneficiary, his life expectancy takes over, and he will be required to make only modest withdrawals at the outset, because he has a much longer life expectancy over which to stretch the withdrawals. And that IRA can function just like a snowball gaining mass as it moves.

A $100,000 IRA earning 8 percent left to a 20-year-old becomes an income stream of $2.8 million over his lifetime if your grandson does nothing more than take minimum withdrawals each year, according to an example calculated by NvestFunds of Boston.

One of the best strategies is to designate your very youngest beneficiaries to inherit your Roth IRA assets, if you have them. Because you won't ever be required to take withdrawals from them during your lifetime, they will have additional years of tax-deferred growth before they are passed on to the next generation. Your beneficiary will be required to make withdrawals, but the withdrawals are tax free, and the younger the beneficiary, the longer they can be stretched out.

A special language is used to designate beneficiaries. Pay attention to it in order to make sure that the people you name get the amount that you want. For example, if you want to provide equally for all your children and their families, you can designate your children as beneficiaries *per stirpes*. That way, if one of your children dies, that share will be passed down to his or her children or beneficiaries. Or, if you want to provide equally for all your children and grandchildren, you can designate them as beneficiaries *per capita*. Each one will get an equal share of your account. If you want to provide only for your children, you can designate that your retirement account proceeds be divided equally among *all my children,* and that covers you even if your family continues to grow after you file your beneficiary form.

◆ **Multiple beneficiaries get new flexibility under new IRS rules.** Before 2001, only one beneficiary's life expectancy governed the rate of required withdrawals from an inherited retirement account: the oldest. And heaven help you if you named your two nephews and an art museum. If you mixed and matched people and places, your nephews' inheritance would have been forced out rapidly, because the art museum doesn't qualify as a designated beneficiary. But thanks to the new IRS rules, which beneficiaries could have begun using as early as 2001, there's more flexibility available going forward. Your heirs have up to September 30 of the year after your death to make certain adjustments to your accounts. No new beneficiaries can be added, but separate accounts can be established for each beneficiary at that time. If there is a beneficiary that doesn't qualify as a designated beneficiary—the art museum in the example above—its share can be distributed. Separate accounts can be established for the other shares—still in the name of the deceased, but with each beneficiary using his or her own life expectancy to determine a withdrawal schedule. It's essential not to change the name of the accounts in this process, or the tax benefits go out the window.

Of course, you can avoid any problem by setting up separate accounts for each beneficiary during your lifetime. But that introduces a new problem: If you want to leave a certain amount to each heir, you'll have to be very careful to follow exactly the same investment strategy with each account, or what starts out as an equal division may not end up that way. The posthumous approach provides an escape hatch, as long as your beneficiaries know it's available.

ABOUT FORMS

IT WOULD BE A MISTAKE to think of your beneficiary form as just one more piece of paper—or one more section to fill out on your account application form. It is a very precious form indeed: *Your beneficiary form is the will for your retirement savings.* If you don't have one, a state court could decide that you have failed to designate a beneficiary and do the job for you. Or, your retirement plan or your IRA may revert to a default option, which is written into most plans and agreements, and that will decide who gets your savings.

Even if you have spelled out your wishes in your will, your beneficiary form takes precedence. You may not be around to observe the fallout, but imagine that you had intended to leave your savings to your elderly mother and instead it ends up with your irresponsible estranged wife, simply because you didn't properly designate a beneficiary.

IN GOOD FORM

BENEFICIARY FORMS are a challenge, according to Kenneth Brier, a Boston attorney who specializes in retirement and estate planning, because there is no such thing as a standardized form. Each financial institution creates its own. I've provided just one example of a form at the end of this section so that you can start to get familiar with what it might ask. The information you write on the form you submit may be too long for the company's computers to handle, and your complete beneficiary designation may not exist in their records. If you have your original form, you're in good shape—as long as your heirs have access to it. You don't want them to have to rely on the records kept by a financial institution over the course of many years, mergers, consolidations, and computer changes. Don't leave the final destination of the money you've saved for retirement to luck. Here's what you should do:

◆ **Complete a beneficiary form for each retirement savings account you have on record.** If a lot of money is at stake and your wishes are lengthy, complicated, or both, you may want to have an estate planning attorney craft a custom beneficiary form. But check to make sure your investment custodian will accept your customized form. Fidelity, for example, will tell you that you must use its standard form and advise you to put any special instructions into your will (which is not the same as relying on your will to designate your beneficiary). But if you are a high-balance customer, you are likely to find someone willing to work with you on your terms. Brier says most companies will work with a customized beneficiary form if you move high enough in the chain of command.

If you use the form provided by a financial institution, make sure you inquire as to how many designations you are allowed. Most will give you room for only two primary beneficiaries and only two contingent beneficiaries on an original form but will allow you to attach additional names on a separate sheet. However, it may be essential to stay within the parameters of their forms to conform to their record keeping systems. Keep multiple copies of the final form in a safe place.

◆ **For each account, designate one or more beneficiaries as well as one or more contingent beneficiaries.** You need protection in case your primary beneficiary does not qualify, typically because he or she has died. Here's the situation you want to avoid: You are divorced and you designate your daughter as your beneficiary. Sadly, you and your daughter perish together. Who gets your retirement plan assets? If your daughter does not have a will, chances are they will go to your ex-spouse because she is the closest relative of your daughter. But let's say your daughter is a teenager or an adult with her own legal will—and a ne'er-

A BENEFICIARY CHECKLIST

1 Choose designated beneficiaries with both your income needs and your beneficiaries' future tax consequences in mind.

2 Choose contingent beneficiaries.

3 Designate your spouse, if he or she will need income. But leave the door open for the assets to be disclaimed.

4 Designate your children or any individual who is younger in order to maximize your income stream while you are alive and to maximize their income stream after you are gone.

5 Remember, the younger your beneficiary, the longer the assets can grow tax-deferred after you are gone.

6 Consider leaving Roth IRA assets to your youngest beneficiaries because the tax benefits are considerable.

7 Complete beneficiary forms for all your retirement savings accounts.

8 Confirm that all beneficiary designations will be honored.

9 Keep multiple copies of all beneficiary forms.

10 Consider a customized beneficiary form created by an estate planning attorney when your assets are significant, your beneficiaries are numerous, or both.

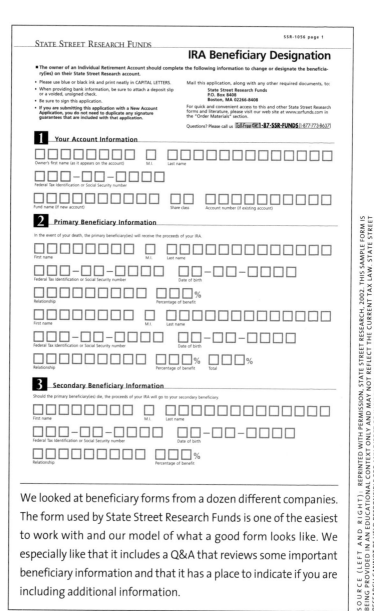

We looked at beneficiary forms from a dozen different companies. The form used by State Street Research Funds is one of the easiest to work with and our model of what a good form looks like. We especially like that it includes a Q&A that reviews some important beneficiary information and that it has a place to indicate if you are including additional information.

do-well boyfriend to whom she has bequeathed all her worldly goods. Now he gets your retirement money, which may not be what you had envisioned during all those years of working and saving. You could have avoided the situation simply by naming a contingent beneficiary on your beneficiary form.

SSR-1056 page 2

Secondary Beneficiary Information (continued)

☐☐☐☐☐☐☐☐ ☐ ☐☐☐☐☐☐☐☐☐☐☐☐☐☐
First name   M.I.   Last name

☐☐☐–☐☐–☐☐☐☐   ☐☐–☐☐–☐☐☐☐
Federal Tax Identification or Social Security number   Date of birth

☐☐☐☐☐☐☐☐☐ ☐☐☐% ☐☐☐%
Relationship   Percentage of benefit   Total

4 Signature(s)

All owners whose names are on the account must sign this application.

☐ **Please check here if you are attaching another sheet with additional beneficiary information. Please note that the total percentage must equal 100%.**

■ **I acknowledge that:**
- I am authorizing the additional services described above.
- I may change my beneficiary(ies) at any time by writing to State Street Research.

☐

Signature (exactly as name appears on new account application or fund statements)

Questions? Please call us Toll-Free ☎ **1-87-SSR-FUNDS** (1-877-773-8637)

5 Questions

We have prepared the following questions and answers to assist you in updating your inherited Individual Retirement Account.

What is the difference between a "primary" and "secondary" beneficiary?
- Your primary beneficiary will receive the proceeds of your account upon your death. The secondary beneficiary will not receive any proceeds unless the primary beneficiary dies first. If the owner has not named a new primary beneficiary, then the secondary beneficiary becomes primary.

What if I name more than one primary or secondary beneficiary?
- The total percentage benefit for both primary and secondary beneficiary designations must total 100%. For example, if you name two primary beneficiaries, unless otherwise stated, each person would receive 50% of the benefit. You have the option of stipulating percentages. If you name five beneficiaries, you may designate them in the following manner: 20%, 15%, 30%, 10%, and 25%—as long as the total designation is 100%.

One of my chosen beneficiaries is a minor, do they need a custodian?
- Yes. All beneficiaries who are minors must have a custodian designated to act on their behalf. You should know that you cannot be named as the custodian for a minor you have listed as beneficiary, but the same adult may be the custodian for multiple beneficiaries.

Do I have to name an individual as a beneficiary?
- You may choose to name a trust or charitable organization as your beneficiary instead of an individual.

Will I receive a confirmation of my beneficiary designation?
- Yes. Your year-end statement will list your beneficiary designations.

How often may I change my beneficiaries?
- No restrictions exist for the number of times you may change your beneficiaries.

Will my beneficiaries remain on the account if I exchange to another fund?
- Yes. Your beneficiary designation applies to your account number and will affect all funds within the account.

STATE STREET RESEARCH
©2002 State Street Research Investment Services, Inc.
One Financial Center, Boston, MA 02111-2690
www.ssrfunds.com
CONTROL NUMBER:(exp0903)SSR-LD

IRA Beneficiary Designation
SSR-1056-0902

◆ **Review your beneficiary form whenever you experience a significant life change.** Examples? If your beneficiary passes away, if you have a new spouse whom you want to add as a beneficiary, or if you have a change of heart about your existing designation. Many single parents put their retirement assets in a trust for the benefit of their minor children, then fail to revisit the situation when their children are grown and the trust is no longer a necessary structure. In fact, it could slow down the disposition of assets if it is left in place.

◆ **To save time and ensure accuracy, change beneficiary forms in person whenever possible.** Changing beneficiaries is easier today than ever before. Thanks to the Internet, you can probably download a beneficiary form from your investment company's website. And thanks to new rules issued by the IRS in 2002, you can change your beneficiary at any time without penalty, even after you have begun the process of taking required minimum withdrawals from your accounts. If you are depending on the U.S. mail to ferry your change-in-beneficiary form, make sure you allow some time for the process to be completed. You'll need to submit new forms for all your accounts, check back to make sure the change has been made to your satisfaction, and keep any written documentation you receive to prove the changes were made.

Two years ago I changed my beneficiary forms on my 401(k), IRAs, and SEP IRA. I submitted one form three times before it was acceptable to the investment company. First I put the name of the trust beneficiary on the wrong line—the form was hard to follow. Then I failed to include an address for the trust. The third time the form was returned to me, I was told that I had to add the year the trust was established, which wasn't stated in the form's instructions. It took nearly four months to complete the process.

PENSION BENEFICIARIES ARE DIFFERENT

THE COMPLICATED CONSIDERATIONS that apply to individual and workplace retirement savings plans generally do not apply to beneficiary designations for a traditional workplace pension plan. If you are covered by such a plan and you are married, you are required to take your spouse's future needs into consideration when you designate a beneficiary and when you select a retirement payout option from your plan. You can name another beneficiary only if your spouse waives his or her rights in writing. Even that option is subject to reconsideration. Your spouse may approve an alternate option during your working years, then have a change of heart before benefits commence. And if rights have been waived, they will need to be waived again if you make any subsequent changes to your beneficiaries.

Taking Your Retirement Money

Your Workplace Pension Plan

Think about your goals and your skills before you choose how you want to take retirement income from a pension plan.

THE NOTION THAT EMPLOYERS have abandoned their pension plans in favor of less costly and more participant-oriented **DEFINED CONTRIBUTION PLANS** such as 401(k)s is one of the abiding myths of retirement in the twenty-first century. It is simply not so. Although small to midsized companies have never been inclined to offer traditional pension plans and the number of large companies offering pension plans has declined in the past twenty-five years, here are the facts according to the Employee Benefit Research Institute:

◆ More than half of all private-sector employees have traditional pension plans.

◆ Nearly 75 percent of all large companies offer traditional pension plans.

◆ More than 90 percent of all state and local government employers offer their workers traditional pension plans.

Most pension plans are still **DEFINED BENEFIT PLANS**, although conversions to alternative hybrid models, such as the **CASH BALANCE PLAN**, are on the rise. Regardless of its type, a defined benefit plan is designed to pay you a retirement benefit on a specified future date, either when you retire or when you leave your employer having negotiated a date to commence benefits earlier than your employer's definition of normal retirement age. (Despite rising life expectancy, 65 years old is still normal for most pension plans.)

The Employee Benefit Research Institute also reports that most aspects of pension payments have changed very little since American Express offered the first company pension back in 1875. Most workers still take their pensions in the form of monthly income. Rigorous laws govern the funding of pension funds that provide the resources for these payouts. Companies build up pension funds over many years and dip into them to purchase **INCOME ANNUITIES** for workers as they retire.

Public employees typically fund their pensions by contributing their own money to an employer's retirement system. That contribution is usually matched by the employer, whether it is a school district, a police unit, or a state government. However, as with Social Security, the amount employees contribute has no direct bearing on the income they end up receiving. In many states, public employees can collect up to 100 percent of their final years' highest wages if they stay long enough. School teachers in thirty-six states have the opportunity to reap this prized benefit.

FIND OUT THE DETAILS

PENSION PLANS VARY, and the only way you can find out about your specific plan is to check with your benefits department or the company that is in charge of administering benefits for your employer. It's a big mistake to assume that your employer will tell you everything you need to know and that all you need to do is sit back and wait for your checks to arrive. If you are entitled to a pension from your employer, here is what you should know—and what you will need to find out:

◆ **Your employer's definition of normal retirement age and the consequences of leaving early—or staying longer.** Although normal retirement age for most employers is 65 (or five years after you start working, whichever comes later), you should find out the date set by your plan. In addition to a definition of normal retirement age, most plans set milestones for early retirement that, with traditional defined benefit plans, involve a lower payout of benefits. That's because traditional pension plans are designed to reward the loyal employee, typically making the years between age 55 and 62 key to achieving the highest possible pension income. Then the table turns, as pension benefits level off and may actually decline at a certain age.

What if you continue to work beyond normal retirement age? Most employers will refuse to pay you pension benefits and a salary at the same time. But it all depends on how your plan is written, says Lou Beckerman of Northeast Planning Services, Inc. He says that employees at some of his clients' firms just continue to show up to work, and there's nothing in their plans to keep them from earning wages and receiving benefits concurrently. Just about anything is possible, and it pays to find out what your plan says.

◆ **Your options for receiving your pension benefits.** Today, many workers are offered two options. One is a stream of regular income for life—usually in the form of a monthly check. The second is a **LUMP SUM DISTRIBUTION**. The lump sum, when it is projected over an individual's life expectancy, would be the equivalent of regular monthly income. For example, if you were entitled to $2,000 a month beginning at age 65 paid to you as a single-life annuity, you might be offered the alternative of $120,000 as a lump sum **DISTRIBUTION**.

Most employees opt for a stream of regular income from a pension annuity and most married employees who opt for regular income also choose the joint-and-survivor option. But the number of employees who take a lump sum distribution has increased as the option has become more available.

How do you know which is right for you? The one important difference is that a pension annuity generally has no intrinsic value beyond your lifetime and that of your spouse, if you are married. If you worked for forty years and you know that your pension could end after three to five years because both you and your spouse have passed away, you may worry that your children and grandchildren will be cheated out of an asset that is rightly theirs.

However, this is not a solid reason to choose a lump sum distribution over a pension annuity. The most important consideration is how you feel about the responsibility of investing and managing a relatively large sum of money or about your ability to choose someone who can carry that responsibility for you. The upside is the chance that your investment performance outdoes the extremely conservative strategy on which your annuity income is based. That gives you the potential for much higher income. The downside is that if it fails, you could end up with an impoverished retirement and no real way of digging your way out. If you are the least bit uncomfortable about the downside, do yourself a favor and opt for the pension annuity.

Of course, if you are married making the choice between an annuity and a lump sum distribution requires that you get your spouse involved. By law, you must elect to receive your pension income as a joint-and-survivor annuity unless your spouse waives his or her rights. The federal government wants to make sure that your spouse has the opportunity to claim a portion of your retirement income. However, this is not true of assets accumulated in a 401(k) or an IRA or any other account where the money is held in a separate account in your name.

Companies differ in what they will offer your spouse if you are the first to die. Typically, he or she will be entitled to anywhere from 50 percent to 75 percent of the amount that would have been paid to you in a single-life annuity. And, if you choose the joint-and-survivor annuity, your payout is smaller during your lifetime than it would be with a single-life annuity. But that seems fair—your employer is covering two lives, not one, in this bargain.

Some joint-and-survivor options promise to increase your benefit up to—or close to—the level of a single-life annuity if your spouse dies first and within a specific period of time. And some options guarantee a certain level of benefits for a set period of time—ten to twenty years, for example—to insure against an untimely death. But if you divorce, there's really no way to cut off your former spouse, although a court would likely take the income into consideration in any settlement.

Clearly, the joint-and-survivor option was created with married couples in mind, but there are dozens of little wrinkles that may be written into your retirement plan. For example, if your spouse passes away, it is most likely that you will have to wait until what would have been his or her earliest possible retirement date before you can collect a pension from that plan. And if you have been married for less than a year, you may be considered unmarried for the purpose of collecting on your new spouse's pension if he or she passes away.

If you work for a small company, you may find that you are entitled to more generous death benefits. For example, some companies offer surviving spouses a 100 percent pension benefit rather than 50 percent or 75 percent, which are more common. And some allow you to name someone other than your spouse as a **BENEFICIARY**.

◆ **The formula used to calculate your benefit.** You may think this is something over which you have no control. However, it's important to know how your benefit is figured, as well as the data that factor into the formula, because it is in these details that mistakes commonly happen (see the sidebar on the following page).

Most formulas are tied to your compensation, the number of years you've worked, or some combination of the two. Your employer may pay you a flat dollar amount for each year of service. Or the payment may be a percentage of your average compensation during your working years multiplied by your years of service. Another method figures a percentage of your highest compensation for your final three to five years' wages. The percentage per year of service dictated by your plan's formula may be as low

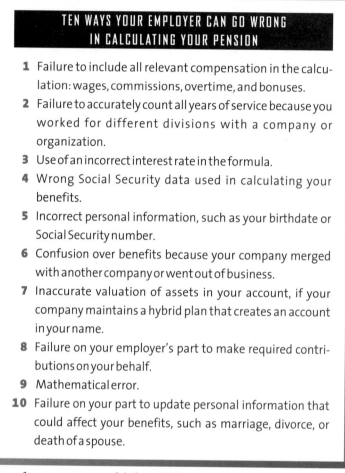

**TEN WAYS YOUR EMPLOYER CAN GO WRONG
IN CALCULATING YOUR PENSION**

1 Failure to include all relevant compensation in the calculation: wages, commissions, overtime, and bonuses.

2 Failure to accurately count all years of service because you
worked for different divisions with a company or
organization.

3 Use of an incorrect interest rate in the formula.

4 Wrong Social Security data used in calculating your
benefits.

5 Incorrect personal information, such as your birthdate or
Social Security number.

6 Confusion over benefits because your company merged
with another company or went out of business.

7 Inaccurate valuation of assets in your account, if your
company maintains a hybrid plan that creates an account
in your name.

8 Failure on your employer's part to make required contributions on your behalf.

9 Mathematical error.

10 Failure on your part to update personal information that
could affect your benefits, such as marriage, divorce, or
death of a spouse.

SOURCE: U.S. DEPARTMENT OF LABOR

as 1 percent or as high as 2.5 percent or more. The average is about 1.45 percent, slightly higher for professional
and technical employees.

Here's how a typical formula works. Say you are retiring
with thirty years of service to your employer and you now
earn $60,000. Your employer's plan uses a formula that
awards you 1.5 percent of your highest annual salary (in
this case, $60,000) for each year of service. That makes
your retirement income $27,000 per year.

What if you choose to receive your pension benefit as a
lump sum distribution? Your employer will figure the present value of the stream of income you would receive over

your life expectancy (based on a currently approved mortality table). Then the benefits people will multiply that by the interest rate on the 30-year U.S. Treasury bond. The low interest rates that have prevailed since the late 1990s present a problem for employers who offer this option to retiring employees. The lower the rate, the higher their payout to you must be to reach the final total amount. As a result, there hasn't been a better time for employees to take a lump sum distribution from a pension plan in the past twenty years.

THE SITUATION FOR employers has become severe enough that the Society of Actuaries sponsored research to identify an alternative. The society doesn't come out and say it's looking for a way to save pension plans some money, but I think you can read between the lines.

Although the 30-year bond has been a standard for some time, employers could pick from a number of different time frames: For example, they could use the rate at the end of the year, at the end of the month, or the average over a several-month period. That flexibility vanished in March 2002, when the IRS announced that it had established a method for determining a single time frame until a longer-term solution can be derived. The IRS will determine and publish the rate of interest on 30-year Treasury securities solely on the basis of the monthly average of the daily determination of yield on the 30-year bond. By the time you read this, a more permanent fix may have been found. (The bottom line is this: If you believe that interest rates are heading downward, it may work to your advantage to put off your retirement date for a few months. Certainly if it looks like interest rates are headed upward, put your retirement date on the calendar now!)

◆ **Entitlement to cost-of-living adjustments.** If you work for a public company, you will be among the fortunate few if your plan calls for increases that reflect the rising cost of living. Less than 5 percent of all pension plans offer them.

Public employees fare better in this regard, as more than half of all public retirement plans build cost-of-living increases into their benefits, typically with a 3 percent cap.

KNOW YOUR RIGHTS

A RETIREE'S WORST FEAR is that the promise to pay a pension will be broken because an employer falls on hard times. Thousands of Polaroid employees came face to face with this reality in the fall of 2001, when the company declared bankruptcy and recently departed employees, most in their late 50s and early 60s, never got the lump sum distributions they were entitled to receive. The good news is that these employees have someone looking out for them in the form of the Pension Benefit Guaranty Corporation (PBGC). Established by Congress in the mid-1970s, the PBGC collects insurance premiums from employers and guarantees individual pension benefits up to $3,579 a month, an amount that is adjusted upward to reflect inflation.

Not all pension plans are covered by the PBGC. Government units and agencies are exempt, as are churches, fraternal associations, or professional service groups with fewer than twenty-five employees.

Recently, the PBGC has announced a nationwide search for thousands of former employees of companies whose pension plans were terminated between 1976 and 1981. According to the law firm of Page/Collins, a class action suit settled in favor of former employees and their survivors could result in payouts of between $10,000 and $12,000 per person. If you think that you or one of your family members may have lost out on benefits during this period, you can call toll free to 866-731-1510 or visit the Page/Collins Settlement website at www.LostPension .net, where you will find a list of companies and other documents.

Though a company's insolvency is the main fear for retirees expecting to collect pension benefits, a merger can also cause some anxious moments. If your firm merges with another while you are working, it may choose to terminate its plan and start up another or adopt the plan of the company with which it merges. If that is the case, you'll be notified of the plan's termination and how and when the distribution of benefits will occur. In most cases, you can expect a lump sum distribution of the estimated current value of your benefits, or the offer of an option to roll them over to the new plan. The IRS takes a very dim view of any employer who tries to reduce or eliminate benefits in the course of a plan change. In other words, your employer can't simply amend its way out of its obligations to existing or retired employees, and the rules are strong enough to pose a serious obstacle to anyone looking for a way around them.

A WORD ABOUT CASH BALANCE PLANS

IT'S ESTIMATED THAT one in five big companies with a defined benefit plan has switched to a cash balance plan—most in the past five years. These hybrid plans are attractive to younger workers because there is a portability feature to them: If you're **VESTED** and leaving for another job, you can actually take some of your accumulated pension benefit with you. Or, if you leave the balance of your vested account behind, it can continue to grow. Cash balance plans are also attractive to companies because they typically end up paying less to workers who remain for twenty or more years. They are least attractive to workers in their 50s and 60s who have been loyal and expect to be rewarded with a generous pension.

Cash balance plans are complicated and confusing, and most companies do a poor job of communicating their impact on employees of differing age groups. A spate of converted plans have ended up in the courts and many of the judgments have been decided in favor of employees. But little compensation has yet been paid back to the employees because of the lengthy appeals process.

Many conscientious companies, mindful that older employees are most likely to be harmed by the conversion, have **GRANDFATHERED** them to receive their benefits under the old plan so they won't be penalized by the change. What can you do if your employer has converted to a cash balance plan and has not made such a gesture? Make sure you understand the plan's impact on your specific situation. Don't accept an explanation you don't fully understand. If you feel that you are being wronged, meet with other employees of similar age and time in service to discuss strategy. You'll need to weigh the merits of a lawsuit against the risks to your current employment status. But don't accept your fate without airing your grievances and raising your questions.

In fact, three agencies may be able to help you address concerns about your pension plan: The Department of Labor, the Internal Revenue Service, and the Department of Justice all can answer questions about the proper administration of pension plans and appropriation of funds. For a summary of what to do if you think rules have been broken, go to www.dol.gov/pwba/public/pubs/protect/guide.

Individual Retirement Savings Accounts

Even if you have never had an IRA, chances are there could be one in your future.

IF YOU HAVE BEEN SAVING for retirement in an individual retirement savings account (IRA), you may already know that these accounts are different from workplace savings plans. Generally speaking, the limits for contributions are lower, there's no benevolent **EMPLOYER MATCH** to your contribution, and the rules that govern withdrawals are much more rigid. Nevertheless, the IRA has been the cornerstone of America's commitment to retirement savings. It was the first plan to make individual tax-deferred retirement savings widely available, and for all its variations, its fundamental concept has changed very little over the years since its introduction in 1978. One IRA variant is also the simplest small business retirement savings plan because it combines the administrative ease of the traditional IRA and the higher contribution limits of a Keogh plan in a special type of IRA called a simplified employee pension (SEP) IRA.

When it comes time to retire, your IRA savings will likely be a valuable source of income. If you have IRAs scattered around at different institutions, it may be a good idea to consolidate them before retirement so that you can simplify the calculations and record keeping you'll be faced with as you get older.

You can withdraw from your IRA penalty free once you are 59½, and you'll be required to begin minimum withdrawals by April 1 of the year after you turn 70½. Compared to the rules for your workplace retirement savings plans, the rules that govern withdrawals from a traditional IRA are far less flexible. (Roth IRAs are different. More about them later.) There are four key differences:

◆ **There is no special category for withdrawals after 55 if you have lost your job as there is with workplace retirement plans.** You must be 59½ to take penalty-free withdrawals from an IRA or follow the rule for taking **SUBSTANTIALLY EQUAL PAYMENTS** (see Number 20).

◆ **There are no special tax breaks.** All withdrawals from IRAs are taxed as **ORDINARY INCOME**. If you have tax-deductible IRAs, you'll pay income tax on the entire amount that you withdraw. If you have nondeductible IRAs, you'll only pay tax on the earnings in your account. The IRS assumes that every time you withdraw money from a nondeductible IRA, part of it is from the taxable portion of the account and part of it is from your original contribution, on which you have already paid income tax. Each year you make a withdrawal, you'll have to file Form 8606 and follow the instructions for figuring your tax.

Because this calculation can be annoying and complicated, it has always made sense to me to keep deductible and nondeductible IRAs in separate accounts. However, now that the tax law allows you to roll over tax-deferred as well as after-tax savings from workplace accounts into an IRA—which means that you won't lose the tax-deferred growth on your after-tax savings—all bets are off. Just face it. This is going to be complicated come tax time. At least help should be forthcoming from your investment company. In the meantime, get a good accountant to do your taxes.

◆ **You must begin required minimum withdrawals by April 1 in the year after you turn 70½, no exceptions.** If you fail to do so, you will be slapped with a 50 percent penalty and you will be required to take the withdrawal. So for example, if you were required to take a $3,000 minimum withdrawal but failed to do so, you'll owe the IRS $1,500 plus you'll still be required to withdraw $3,000. (You can postpone these withdrawals from workplace savings accounts if you're still working, as long as you do not own 5 percent of the company or more.) Because IRA custodians will have to report all account owners required to take minimum distributions going forward, most companies have decided to alert customers when this deadline approaches. That may help keep more individuals out of the penalty box.

◆ **You cannot continue to contribute to an IRA after age 70.** If you ignore this rule and continue to make contributions, you will be subject to a 6 percent penalty tax on the excess contribution. You will also owe that 6 percent on the amount of the contribution, plus all earnings attributable to the excess amount for every year that it is in your account.

ROTH IRAS ARE DIFFERENT

ALL THE RULES ABOUT TAXES and withdrawals go out the window for a Roth IRA as long as you satisfy two key requirements: Your Roth IRA is five or more years old and you are age 59½ when you begin to withdraw. Actually, the amount you've contributed to your Roth IRA is always available because you've already paid taxes on it.

With a Roth IRA, you won't ever be required to take a withdrawal in your lifetime if you choose not to. Your heirs will have to follow the rules for withdrawals over their life expectancies. And you can continue to contribute as long as you have earned income. There's no age limit for contributing to a Roth IRA if you meet income eligibility requirements.

ROLLOVER IRA: ONE LAST STOP
FOR YOUR RETIREMENT SAVINGS?

ONCE YOU REACH NORMAL retirement age or once you leave your last employer, you will have to make some decisions about your workplace retirement savings. Most plans will force your hand, asking you to choose a **SYSTEMATIC WITHDRAWAL PLAN** (see Number 6), cash in your savings, or move it out of the plan. After normal retirement age, you're no longer their responsibility, so it's time to get you off the books.

Cashing in is a tax nightmare, so if you are going to move the money out you have two choices: Rolling over to a qualified annuity (see Number 17) or a rollover IRA. Some call it a "conduit IRA" because the process preserves the tax deferral of the previous plan as it moves into the IRA.

A rollover IRA is really just like any other traditional IRA. However, instead of being used primarily to accumulate savings over time, a rollover IRA is designed to receive the assets you've been accumulating in other retirement savings plans. Sort of like the place of last resort when your money has finally been kicked out of your other plans. Savings that goes into it keeps its tax-deferred status, and it's taxed as ordinary income when it comes out. There's virtually no limit to the amount you can roll over to an IRA. It's not unheard of for successful workers, who have accumulated millions of dollars in company stock in their 401(k), **PROFIT SHARING**, and **EMPLOYEE STOCK OWNER-SHIP PLANS**, to roll the entire amount over to an IRA to get access to a broader range of investments for diversification.

Once your savings finds its way to an IRA, you can take charge as the investment manager and expand into a broader range of investments or streamline to reflect a simple mix of major asset classes. Or, you can hire professional help to manage it for you. But you can also relax, because an IRA can be the last stop on the savings train. The only operational detail you have to worry about is taking your required minimum withdrawals after age 70½. And now that companies will be required to report this information to you, it should help you avoid a penalty for not taking a distribution when you should.

If you have questions about your IRA or any aspect of rolling over to an IRA, converting to a Roth IRA, or **RECHARACTERIZING** an IRA contribution, you can find answers from a panel of tax and retirement experts at www.irahelp.com. The site belongs to Ed Slott, a CPA from Rockville Centre, New York, who is the nation's leading expert on IRAs. Slott publishes a monthly newsletter, *Ed Slott's IRA Advisor,* and delivers his practical and intelligent advice with wit and good humor.

Small Business Retirement Savings Plans

Similar rules, but fewer protections, apply to small business retirement plans.

ALTHOUGH SMALL BUSINESSES employ nearly 40 percent of all workers in the private sector, the majority offer no retirement benefits. So consider yourself fortunate if you work for a company with fewer than 100 employees and you are covered by a retirement savings or pension plan.

Small business retirement plans usually fall into three categories: IRA variations, Keogh plans, and 401(k)s. Keogh plans can be designed as **PROFIT SHARING**, money purchase, or **DEFINED BENEFIT PENSION PLANS**.

When you work for a small business, pay special attention as you count down to retirement. If you have been saving for retirement in a payroll deduction IRA or a SEP IRA, your money is in a separate account with your name on it, and there's not much to worry about. For the purpose of withdrawals and taxes, the same rules apply to small business IRAs as apply to individual IRAs (see Number 7). If your plan is a Keogh or a 401(k), it is a **QUALIFIED PLAN**—and as such, it must follow the same rules regarding withdrawals, taxes, and penalties that apply to larger companies' plans (see Number 6).

But there *are* official as well as certain unofficial differences that you should know about. The biggest difference is an official one: The Department of Labor does not require, nor does it conduct, independent audits of retirement plans in companies with 100 or fewer employees. As a result, there's more opportunity for abuse among small company plans.

That said, there is no evidence that employees at small companies report more abuse, but it is worth knowing the possibilities. For example, because small companies are often slim on staffing, an owner may serve as the trustee of the company's plan. That affords the small business owner direct access to the funds deposited in employee accounts with the plan's custodian. Typically, a larger company would hand off that responsibility to an independent organization. Even if your employer is scrupulously ethical, he or she may be slow or disorganized or simply pulled in too many directions, and these habits can have a negative impact on the way things get done with your plan. For example, the process of cashing someone out of a plan may not go smoothly because it is only an occasional, or even a rare, thing.

The timing of your account valuation when you leave the company is another big difference between large and small company plans. The majority of large companies value accounts daily because they have sophisticated record keeping systems. Your small company employer may value your account once a quarter—or even more common, once a year.

Think about what that means: If you retire as of December 31 and your plan is valued as of December 31, you'll have a pretty good idea of what to expect when you **ROLL OVER** your 401(k) and profit sharing plan into an IRA. But what if you chose to leave on May 1? You'll probably have to wait until the next December 31 to get your hands on your money—and it will be valued on that date.

Wrinkles like these certainly make retiring from a small company more of a crapshoot. And it points to the need to find out the details of your company's valuation policy while you are still in the early planning stages for retirement.

If you are a highly compensated employee in a small company, here's another thing to keep in mind: Your plan may offer the option of a **LUMP SUM DISTRIBUTION**, but it may not have the resources to make good on that offer if you are entitled to a very high amount. You could find yourself forced to take an annuity payout. And if that has an impact on your postretirement plans, you may be sorry that you didn't inquire sooner.

If your small business retirement plan owns unusual assets, such as real estate, artwork, gold, a limited partnership, or closely held stock, your share in these items will have to be valued and sold before you can take it—another reason to give yourself plenty of time to count down to retirement, and plenty of notice to your employer.

The higher volatility of small businesses suggests one strategy for departing employees: Don't leave your pension and or/retirement savings behind. Take it, on your first opportunity. Roll it over to an IRA or qualified annuity. Without some of the protection afforded to larger companies, it's simply too risky to leave it behind.

And if you are the sole proprietor with a Keogh plan—a doctor, lawyer, florist, or dog groomer—you have a different reason to roll your savings over to an IRA as soon as you are ready to retire. Plan rules require that your **BENEFICIARY**, if it is anyone other than your spouse, withdraw all the money in short order and pay taxes on it. What a waste of an opportunity to stretch withdrawals out over your beneficiary's life expectancy, preserve tax deferral, and postpone taxes. Recently the IRS agreed to bend those rules for the beneficiaries of a $2 million Keogh—a good thing to know, but not something anyone else can count on. If your beneficiaries found themselves in the same situation, they would need their own IRS private letter ruling and they would pay a handsome sum for it. Do them a favor and plan ahead.

Know the Rules for Rollovers and Withdrawals

Rollovers and Withdrawal Options for Workplace Retirement Savings Plans

You have more options for tax savings and control if you understand the eligibility rules and deadlines.

WHEN YOU LEAVE YOUR JOB, no matter what the reason, you have important choices to make about your workplace retirement savings. Most employers offer three basic choices to departing or retiring employees. Typically, you can leave your savings where it is, as long as you have at least $5,000 in your account; withdraw the money; or roll the money over into an IRA, a qualified annuity, or to another employer's retirement plan. Most workplaces will offer workshops or seminars that spell out your choices. These can be informative. But be skeptical if the presentations come from any of the investment companies that currently manage your retirement savings plan. Although most will have to keep their program nonpromotional on the surface—they won't be able to baldly pitch ABC mutual fund or XYZ annuity—they can still build a fair amount of bias into their presentations. Larger providers with broad product offerings usually present the most reliable information because they figure they have a shot at getting your money no matter what you choose. Insurance companies are the most heavy-handed because they simply can't resist making their options look a little better than the others.

If you decide to leave your savings where they are to continue to grow **TAX DEFERRED**, ask about:

◆ restrictions that might be placed on access to your money going forward

◆ limitations on transactions and/or increases in fees that will apply to you as a departing employee that did not apply when you were working

◆ the date when you must take action by withdrawing the money, rolling it over, or turning it into a stream of periodic payments, which is sometimes called a **SYSTEMATIC WITHDRAWAL PLAN**.

You should be able to get answers to these questions from your employer's benefits representative, who may be someone in your company—or someone in a benefits management company to which your employer has outsourced these responsibilities. Answers may be included in the annual benefits report that many large companies send out. Certainly, the information must appear in your employer's official **PLAN DOCUMENT**. Plan documents aren't exactly light reading; nevertheless, consider asking your employer for a summary of your plan document—which, by law, must be updated each year and available for the asking. Look for the answers to these questions, making sure that you understand them and that they jibe with what you are told by the benefits spokesperson.

A former employee *doesn't* want to find

◆ that you might have limited ability to change your investment options—or that you might have to follow some cumbersome formula imposed by the company. For example, because employers are loath to incur charges for individuals who no longer work for them, they may restrict you to two transactions a year. Or they may require that any transaction you make involve at least 50 percent of your savings.

◆ that you have to pay an annual fee that is too high to justify your continued participation. According to John Doyle, who heads retirement services for T. Rowe Price in Baltimore, this practice is virtually unknown among large company plans. In fact, because it's in the best interest of the investment company that manages your employer's plan to hold on to your money even after you've moved on, they may actually absorb the cost.

◆ that there is a deadline that could lock your money into the plan until you reach retirement age if you don't act within a certain number of days to take the money out, either as a withdrawal or a rollover. Doyle points out that some plans will give you thirty days to decide what to do with your retirement plan savings. If you do nothing, you can't touch the money until you have reached the plan's designated retirement age—typically age 65. This is pretty scary. And although it may not be common practice, it can make all the difference knowing that it is your company's practice.

These may not be automatic reasons to leave the plan, but they demand consideration. One more thing: If you work for a small business, it's almost always a good idea to move your retirement savings along with you. Because small companies receive less protection from the Department of Labor, they offer more opportunities for improprieties.

REASONS TO LEAVE MONEY IN YOUR EMPLOYER'S PLAN

ARE THERE GOOD REASONS to leave your savings with a former employer? Yes. Certainly, if you have access to an investment manager or a fund that is closed to the public outside of your plan, and you value that choice, you should consider leaving the money where it is. For example, former Fidelity employees have access to the management talent of Neal Miller of Fidelity New Millennium Fund only through their 401(k) plan or through another 401(k) plan that offers Fidelity funds. If you roll your savings over to an IRA at Schwab, your assets will be sold and you're out of luck with regard to Miller: New Millennium Fund has been closed to new investors for years.

Your savings may also be safer in your employer's plan. Not because the investments are protected from the whims of the market, but because retirement plan savings are accorded protection from creditors that does not necessarily extend to an IRA and most certainly does not extend to a regular, taxable account. In fact, now that the rules have become more flexible on rollovers, some financial experts see an opportunity for workers to roll all of their other retirement savings into the 401(k) of their last employer. You can use it as your primary retirement income account and to maximize protection against creditors and any other claims. However, before you start down that path, you must make sure that your employer has changed its plan to allow the transaction—just because Congress says a company *can* do it does not mean that they *must* do it—and weigh the tradeoffs of being tied to your former employer's plan through all its future changes.

In many very large companies, T. Rowe Price's Doyle says, it has become common practice to encourage former employees to stay in the plan—sort of a new wave of paternalism from old-line companies such as automakers, chemical manufacturers, and consumer products companies. If your employer is going out of its way to provide incentives to stay put, why not consider them, especially if you have other ongoing relationships with the firm—health care benefits or the expectation of a traditional pension payout.

WHEN TIME'S UP

ONCE YOU REACH AN AGE designated by your employer's plan—usually 65—your employer can ask you to leave the plan or to begin a systematic withdrawal program that will be based either on your life expectancy or an amount of money you want to receive at regular intervals. This can be a perfectly reasonable choice, but take care to verify exactly what you are getting. A systematic withdrawal program is nothing more than a plan for withdrawing a certain amount of money every month, every quarter, or even once a year based on your life expectancy.

According to John D. Begley, CFP at T. Rowe Price, here's how that might work if you have $100,000 invested in three mutual funds—50 percent in stocks, 30 percent in bonds, and 20 percent in a money market fund. Using the

Single Life Expectancy Table (which appears on page 186) that drives a lot of financial planning calculations, and assuming a total annual return of 7 percent each and every year, you would receive a check for $397 every month beginning at age 65. If your investments returned more than 7 percent annually, you would still be receiving your $397 monthly at age 90. Plus, your account would be worth more than $250,000. Of course, accounts sometimes lose money, as investors have discovered in the past few years, so keep that in mind before you start thinking about spending that $250,000 in advance.

There is more than one way to arrange for this type of withdrawal program. You can choose to have your percentage increased slightly every year to offset inflation. Or, you can take a different tack and request a certain dollar amount of money from the account. Most individuals use this specific dollar approach to take out *more* money than a systematic plan would have called for. The risk there is that your money may run out during your lifetime.

If the amount is less than the systematic amount, your account value should remain higher in the early years. But after age 70½, you'll be required to take IRS-mandated minimum withdrawals, which are based on the Uniform Lifetime Table (page 105), and you will draw down your account at a slightly different pace than under the first scenario.

When you choose a systematic withdrawal plan, make sure you aren't buying an annuity posing as a systematic withdrawal plan. Financial planner and television commentator Ginger Applegarth stumbled onto this practice in the course of her research several years ago. She discovered that one large investment company that manages retirement savings plans offers departing employees the option of a systematic withdrawal program that is actually an annuity. On one hand, you're not going to outlive your money. But once you sign on, the money is no longer yours and you can forget any notion of growth or rising income.

There may be nothing wrong with an annuity—it's often a very good choice for at least some portion of your retirement income. But you don't want to be misled into thinking you're opting for one selection and receiving another.

If you decide to withdraw some or all of your money, you'll owe federal—and in most cases state—income tax on the amount you take in the year that you withdraw it. What's more, because it is added to your other income, it could send you into a much higher tax bracket unless you are entitled to one of the special tax treatments discussed in detail in Number 11. If you decide to take this route, be sure to investigate any special tax breaks that are available to you before you touch even *one dollar* of your accounts. Why? Because some of the special tax breaks have eligibility requirements that can be affected if you start tinkering around with withdrawals on a piecemeal basis. David Foster, a partner at the Cincinnati advisory firm of Foster & Motley, has seen this situation too many times in his twenty years advising workers leaving Procter & Gamble, a company with a wonderful **PROFIT SHARING PLAN**. "Excited about retirement, a fellow takes $20,000 out in December to buy a new car, retires in January—and discovers that he has just lost out on an opportunity to save money on his taxes because of the partial withdrawal he took the previous year," says Foster.

And before you request a withdrawal—in fact, before you set a retirement date—find out when your plan is valued. Doyle says that only 65 percent of all of today's workplace retirement savings plans are valued daily. That means 35 percent have quarterly or—more common for small companies—yearly valuation. Small companies are the ones most likely to operate with annual valuation.

Are there good reasons for withdrawing all of the money when you leave your employer? If you're leaving for another job, the answer is simply "no." Even if it's a small amount of money, you will be giving up the potential to multiply it ten or twenty times before retirement, especially if you are still relatively young. But what if you are leaving and you *don't* have another job—and you're also too young to retire? Consider it the last resort in a true emergency, but if you have exhausted other reasonable possibilities—an equity loan for your home, for example— it's better to use your retirement savings than to rack up credit card debt.

If you are retiring and you have a business investment in mind—buying a McDonald's franchise, for example— that qualifies as a reason to withdraw. Buying an income-producing condo? Maybe. You're giving up a future of tax-deferred growth and paying the IRS as soon as the money hits your wallet. But if you have a backup plan if your new investment fails, it could be just the source of funds you need.

If you decide to **ROLL OVER** your savings into an IRA, your money stays under the umbrella of tax deferral and you take over as the manager of your assets. By law, your employer must offer you the option of a rollover to an IRA or a new employer's retirement plan. Your new employer, however, can place certain restrictions on your money. Be sure to ask before you set the ball in motion.

In a **DIRECT ROLLOVER**, no taxes are owed, nothing is withheld in anticipation of taxes, and no penalties are incurred. The money is **TRANSFERRED** from your em-ployer's plan to an IRA at a financial institution of your choosing or to your new employer's plan, and the money never touches your hands. Here are seven other things you should know about rollovers—and the choices and con-siderations that come along with them.

A ROLLOVER IS A TWO-STEP PROCESS THAT INVOLVES YOU, YOUR EMPLOYER, AND A NEW FINANCIAL INSTITUTION

YOU MUST SELECT a **FINANCIAL SUPERMARKET**, a mutual fund company, a full-service broker, a bank, or an insur-ance company. Contact the place you have decided to move your money to. Fill out an account application, which you may be able to do online. You'll have to choose new investment options and designate **BENEFICIARIES** as part of the initial paperwork. Then, you must go to your employer to request a rollover of your account savings. You'll need to provide the name of the financial institution where you have opened your rollover IRA and your new account number.

Most big employers are accustomed to this process and should make it fairly easy for you. But remember, you are the person with a vested interest in speed and accuracy, and only you can make sure the rollover happens the way you want it to. Ask your employer to identify the steps your request will take before your money is actually sent to its new home and an estimate of how much time each step will take. Then, mark your checkpoints on your calendar and get in touch with your contact if the process bogs down at any point. This is definitely a squeaky wheel situation. Steve Mitchell, a Boston-based consultant to investment companies on retirement matters, says that the process should take three to five weeks from start to finish if everything goes according to script. A rollover between the investment company that manages your workplace retirement plan and that same company's rollover IRA can take less than forty-eight hours!

What could make the process break down?

◆ **an overworked administrator** who has a backlog of requests at your place of work, or a relatively low-tech computer infrastructure, which may may mean there's more need for hands-on involvement at decision points that are handled electronically by other firms. Be sure to check in each week to keep your request moving.

◆ **a messy situation**—an outstanding loan that needs to be settled, multiple accounts that include before- and after-tax money and positions in company stock, a **QUALIFIED DOMESTIC RELATIONS ORDER (QDRO)** that means someone else has claim to a portion of your savings, or exotic investments that may not be highly liquid.

◆ **an inexperienced financial institution** on the receiving end. Although I hesitate to make this generalization, we concluded from a telephone survey of top providers in every category of financial institutions that big companies know more than small ones; the easiest place to roll over to is a company that serves self-directed investors; brokers still want to put one of their financial advisers between you and the process; and banks are way, way behind in terms of knowledge of the process and service provided— even the big ones.

That said, just about everybody is better at the rollover process than they were four years ago when I did my first research on companies and their rollover operations. Some of the largest mutual fund companies and financial supermarkets have created separate business units and have trained their representatives to handle most rollover requests. Some companies have created rollover specialists who take over when a transaction is complex or the dollars involved are substantial. Schwab, for example, assigns a personal rollover assistant if your account is worth $100,000 or more. Fidelity, Vanguard, and Schwab will let you apply for the account online. Everything, right down to the signature, can be electronic.

WITH A ROLLOVER, YOU CAN CONSOLIDATE MONEY FROM MORE THAN ONE RETIREMENT PLAN INTO A SINGLE ACCOUNT IF YOU HAVE LEFT 401(k) or 403(b) money with former employers, or if you are expecting a **LUMP SUM DISTRIBU-TION** from a traditional pension plan, you can roll all of that money into your IRA. You can even combine regular IRA money with a rollover IRA and after-tax contributions to an employer's plan with before-tax money—thanks to a change in the tax laws in 2001. But this flexibility is a double-edged sword. On one hand, it will ensure that all of your retirement savings continue to enjoy tax-deferred growth. However, once you start aggregating before- and after-tax money into a single account, it will make your tax computations a lot harder when you begin to take money out of the consolidated account. (You'll have to appropriate your withdrawals into "before" and "after" tax portions—get your accountant on board for help.) One more thought: Because you could end up with a mountain of paperwork, you might want to do multiple rollovers one at a time. Open your rollover IRA, roll over the savings from your last employer. Then, move on to the next only when the money from your last employer is in the account. Finish one before you start the next.

YOU TYPICALLY HAVE A BROADER CHOICE OF INVESTMENTS WITH A ROLLOVER IRA

THE AVERAGE WORKPLACE savings plan has about ten investment options. Some have as few as four. As a departing employee, you may not have access to the full list of options available to active employees. But in step with the paternalism that some large companies are once again exhibiting toward their employees, some plans actually offer departing employees access to a broader range of choices. However, it's hard to imagine that you could do better than a rollover to an IRA at a financial supermarket, where you could get access to thousands of funds and individual securities as well as CDs and annuities.

Now, more doesn't necessarily mean better. But along with a broad range of investment options, you may also find a wider range of services, online tools and calculators, and educational information. Those items are often in limited supply when you leave your retirement savings in your employer's plan. As a former employee, you may find you continue to have access to some items—the company website, for example—but are cut off from other educational and informational goodies that were available to you when you were an active worker.

YOUR WORKPLACE SAVINGS PLAN INVESTMENTS WILL PROBABLY BE SOLD BEFORE THEY ARE ROLLED OVER

THIS MAY COME as a surprise, but think about it: If you own Fidelity funds in your 403(b) and roll them over to a Fidelity IRA, no problem. But if you choose to roll over the Oppenheimer funds you own in your 401(k) to an IRA at

T. Rowe Price, there's no such match. In this case, T. Rowe Price's Doyle says, your funds will be valued at the closing price of the day they finalize paperwork and a matching purchase transaction, for the funds you select, will be executed. There should be no cost to you involved in the transaction. You'll receive a written confirmation of both transactions, but you don't have much control over when the transfers will happen, except to the extent that you choose when to initiate the process.

Most IRA custodians can handle a rollover of company stock—there's no reason why that should be sold—but be sure to ask. The new financial institution will need to have a brokerage capability, which some smaller or more specialized institutions do not have.

If you have any unusual assets in your 401(k), you should talk with the financial institution you choose about how they will be valued and liquidated. This can be dicey, for example, if you own **RESTRICTED STOCK** or an asset such as a limited partnership in your plan. If you find yourself in this situation, get the help of a financial adviser and give yourself plenty of extra time—at least six months—to work through the process.

YOU DON'T HAVE TO ROLL YOUR ASSETS OVER TO AN IRA

YOU CAN ALSO ROLL OVER to a qualified annuity at an insurance company. An annuity may be a good choice for some, all, or none of your retirement savings. Your decision depends on a variety of factors relating to your income needs and your attitude about risk, topics that are taken up in more detail in Numbers 16 and 17. Some of the biggest and most established names in insurance, such as Hartford or Prudential, offer annuities with a very broad range of bells and whistles—which also have significant charges associated with them. Many mutual fund companies have also established insurance companies within their complexes so that they can sell a rollover annuity, which is likely to be more basic and come at a much lower fee. Teachers, professors, and hospital workers who have accumulated their savings in annuities managed by TIAA-CREF have an easy rollover into an **INCOME ANNUITY** with this big name provider. But if you fall into this category, make sure you understand your choices: You aren't required to choose an annuity for your rollover—and, as with any rollover, you aren't required to keep it with the firm that has managed your savings during your working years.

A ROLLOVER IS A NECESSARY INTERIM STEP IF YOU WISH TO CONVERT TO A ROTH IRA

YOU CAN'T GO DIRECTLY from your workplace retirement savings plan to a Roth IRA. But once you've made the transfer of assets to a rollover IRA, it's just one more piece of paperwork to convert to a Roth—if you are prepared to pay income tax on the full amount you convert and if you are eligible. Your income can't exceed $100,000 in the year of the **CONVERSION**, whether you are single or married and filing jointly. However, income should not be a barrier to eligibility. Even if you were an aging rock star, you would simply have to discipline yourself to make no more than $100,000 on January 1 of the year you plan to retire and call it a day. Or a year. You get the picture.

There is one way to get caught by the eligibility rules that you may not be able to get around: If you wait until the year you turn 70½ to think about a Roth IRA conversion and you have so much money in your retirement account that your first **REQUIRED MINIMUM DISTRIBUTION** (the official amount that the IRS requires you to take out of your retirement savings each year after 70½) puts you over the $100,000 mark, you can kiss your Roth conversion goodbye—at least until you can lower your income, which with a very large account may not be possible. If your required minimum distribution plus your income push you over the $100,000 mark, you're stuck, because both count against the eligibility limit. Congress has passed a provision that will exclude required minimum distributions from the eligibility test beginning in

2005, but you can avoid a problem in the near term by playing it safe.

The key attraction of the Roth IRA is that it offers the opportunity for tax-free income after money has been in your account for five years and you have reached the magic age of 59½. Any income you take from a Roth IRA is tax free and any income your heirs receive after you're gone is also tax free. There's another, equally compelling but not-so-obvious Roth advantage: You aren't required to make withdrawals from your account—at least not in your lifetime.

It's important to grasp both the income eligibility strategy and the Roth IRA's key advantages, because conversion is most attractive to individuals with very high account balances and other retirement resources who are unlikely to need all their retirement savings in their own lifetimes. The potential for tax-free income and the opportunity to leave your Roth IRA assets untouched during your lifetime make a Roth IRA the ideal estate planning tool. And that's primarily why you should consider a Roth IRA conversion. If you're going to need your IRA for retirement income, it makes little sense to accelerate your tax bill, which is all you'll achieve with a Roth IRA conversion: You'll owe income tax at your **ORDINARY INCOME** tax rate on the entire amount of the conversion in the year you execute the transaction. That would make the IRS happy, but it doesn't do much for you. What's more, you would be putting a padlock on any earnings on those assets for five years and you could need other resources to tap during the five-year waiting period before your Roth IRA is completely available to you tax free.

Some investment companies have gone to great lengths to create extraordinary hypothetical examples that are designed to demonstrate that you can earn back the money you paid out early in taxes by getting great performance from your investments, which then continue to compound tax free. But it takes an extraordinary investment environment and incredible good fortune to make these figures look good. You should also be able to pay your taxes out of other, nonretirement funds. A more likely result is that you will take some of your **DISTRIBU-TION** to pay your taxes. Your retirement savings will shrink on their way into a Roth IRA—plus it will be "hands off" your earnings for five years. And if you don't earn the boffo return that is required to make this work out in your favor, you come out behind. There's simply not enough in it for most individuals nearing retirement age to convert unless they have estate planning in mind.

Of course, if you expect to leave a significant portion of your retirement savings for your heirs, you may think you're off the hook with the federal estate tax set to expire in 2010. However, few financial planners expect that will ever happen because Congress has to vote on it in 2011 or before in order to make it permanent. Besides, the estate tax in the years leading up to 2010 remains steep, although modestly lower than before and applicable to fewer inherited dollars.

WHEN YOU ROLL OVER YOUR RETIREMENT SAVINGS INTO AN IRA, YOU ARE IN CHARGE

IF THAT'S NOT WHAT you had in mind, before you take on this onerous process, get a financial adviser involved to handle the rollover for you. However, if you're comfortable in this role, put a plan in place to give it the attention it deserves. I call this becoming CEO of Your Retirement, Inc. You need an investment strategy, an income strategy, and a plan for reviewing both at regular intervals. (More on strategies in Numbers 15 and 16.) If you have a serious chunk of money in your rollover IRA, the worst thing you can do is to attack it piecemeal—taking money out willy-nilly, moving investments around when the markets get scary or you get fed up with technology stocks. There is a lot about investing that you can't control, but the job that you assume when you put yourself in charge of your assets has as much to do with process as with inspired investment decisions. You can lose the war if you don't win these battles from the start.

One more thing about a rollover: Although it is *often* the best strategy for your retirement savings, it isn't *always* the best strategy. If you own a large position in your employer's stock in your retirement plan and if you have been accumulating it over many years, you may be able to do much better tax-wise to take the stock **IN KIND**— it won't be sold as you move it into an account outside your employer's plan. This is a special situation. Look for more information in Number 21.

10

Required Withdrawals from Your Retirement Savings Plans

You must begin minimum withdrawals from most accounts at 70½. But there are some ways to delay.

THINK OF THE YEARS between 59½ and 70½ as the sweet spot of your retirement savings. You can do virtually anything you want with your money without penalty, and generally without paperwork. You can withdraw as much or as little as you want—although for most retirees, it's a better idea to tap other resources and leave tax-deferred savings to continue to grow as long as you can.

But when you reach 70½, the IRS says, "Enough already!" Even if you don't need to tap your accounts and would just as soon let them continue to grow **TAX DEFERRED**, the IRS wants to collect the unpaid taxes. It has waited patiently, and now it's payback time. At 70½, you must begin taking annual **REQUIRED MINIMUM DISTRIBUTIONS** from your traditional, rollover, and SEP IRAs, and from your workplace savings plans.

A FEW EXCEPTIONS

IF YOU'RE STILL WORKING, you may postpone your required withdrawals until April 1 of the year after you leave the workforce, so long as you're not one of the big guys. If you own 5 percent or more of the company, the 70½ date applies to you. This exception has long applied to government and church workers but was extended to workers in public companies in the 1990s.

There are two more exceptions: There are no required minimum withdrawals in your lifetime for your Roth IRAs, and if you have accumulated savings in a 403(b) plan, you can postpone withdrawals on the balance of your account as of December 31, 1986, until you are 75. Here's what you'll need to do:

◆ Establish your December 31, 1986, account balance. Only that amount, and none of the subsequent earnings on it, qualifies for postponed withdrawals—and only if your account custodian keeps records of the pre- and post-1987 balances.

◆ Subtract your 1987 balance each year before you calculate your required minimum distribution.

◆ If you take more than your required amount, it will count against your 1987 balance and reduce the **GRAND-FATHERED** amount until it is exhausted.

◆ If you roll your entire account into an IRA, you'll forfeit the option to defer any distributions until you are 75. After age 75, you'll figure required minimum distributions on your total account balances.

WHEN TO TAKE YOUR FIRST REQUIRED MINIMUM DISTRIBUTION

YOUR FIRST REQUIRED minimum distribution is for the year in which you turn 70½. However, you aren't required to take your first withdrawal until April 1 of the year *after* you turn 70½. That's what the IRS calls your **REQUIRED BEGIN-NING DATE**. If you wait until April 1 to take your first withdrawal, you'll be required to take a second withdrawal in that same calendar year—some time before December 31.

Confused already? Say you turn 70 on May 1, 2003. Counting out six months, you will turn 70½ on November 1, 2003. Your first required minimum distribution would be due by April 1, 2004. You'll also be required to take a minimum distribution for the calendar year 2004 by December 31. Then, in each calendar year that follows, you'll be required to take a minimum distribution until you have exhausted your retirement savings.

So much for the "when" of required minimum distributions. That was the easy part. You also need to know how much to withdraw in order to satisfy the IRS definition of "minimum"—and you need to know how to figure out subsequent withdrawals because they change every year.

Thanks to a recent move by the IRS, this calculation has just gotten much easier. As more money began to accumulate in tax-advantaged IRAs and 401(k)s, it was becoming clear to the IRS that the complex rules and regulations that had been in place since 1987 were causing serious problems for retirees. Many made elections they didn't understand, and their heirs suffered for it. Even financial professionals found the rules baffling. In 2001, the IRS proposed sweeping changes, which were finalized in 2002.

HOW TO CALCULATE YOUR REQUIRED MINIMUM DISTRIBUTIONS

GONE ARE THE COMPLEX formulas and confusing elections! And in most instances, the **NEW RULES** also lower the amount you are required to take, which can translate into a huge tax savings. There's also greater flexibility in naming **BENEFICIARIES** to your accounts, and that flexibility extends to your heirs, who will find it easier to stretch out withdrawals from the accounts they inherit.

It would take too many pages to describe the old rules—and what's the point? They are out. The new rules are in. Even retirees who were taking distributions under the **OLD RULES** are entitled to a fresh start. Here's what you need to know to figure out your required minimum distributions.

◆ **Get the value of your retirement savings on December 31 of the previous year.** This assumes that your accounts are valued on December 31. If you have money in a **QUALIFIED PLAN** that values its accounts once a year and not on December 31, you'll use the last balance you have for that account. Add up the value of all your accounts—individual retirement accounts and workplace retirement savings accounts. Do not include any money that you have set aside in **TAX-DEFERRED ANNUITIES** outside of your workplace. You won't be required to take withdrawals from them until you are 90. And don't include any Roth IRA.

◆ **Find your life expectancy on the IRS-approved Uniform Lifetime Table.** (The IRS calls this your **APPLICABLE DISTRIBUTION PERIOD** or **ADP**. I call it your life expectancy because that's what it is. You'll find it in Table A on page 105.) Under the old rules, the age of your beneficiary was a factor at some point in how much money came out of your accounts. Under the new rules, the age of your beneficiary is irrelevant unless you are married and your spouse is more than ten years younger than you are and also your **SOLE BENEFICIARY**. Then, you have the option of using your joint life expectancies to calculate your required minimum distributions, which was also true under the old rules. (See Table B on pages 106–107.)

It's really pretty simple. You take the value of your savings, find your life expectancy on the appropriate table, and divide your savings by your life expectancy. Here's an example: Say that you turned 70½ in 2002 and you will be required to take your first distribution by April 1, 2003. You have an IRA, worth $100,000 on December 31, 2002. Your life expectancy for the year in which you turned 70½ is 27.4 years. (Remember, if you wait until April 1, your first required withdrawal is actually for the previous year.)

Your first required minimum withdrawal is $3,649. Compared to the old rules, your required minimum distribution—and your income tax—have been nearly halved.

If you waited to take your first required minimum distribution until April 1, 2003, you will use the same December 31, 2002, account balance to figure your second distribution. However, you will subtract the first distribution before you divide by your life expectancy (which at 71 has dropped to 26.5 years) to arrive at your required minimum distribution for 2003.

In fact, you should think about your tax situation before you decide to take the IRS up on its generous offer to postpone your first required minimum distribution until April 1. If taking two distributions in the same tax year shoots you up into a higher income tax bracket, you may be better off taking your first required withdrawal in the calendar year that you turn 70½. Generally speaking, your account balance has to be significant in order for this to matter, but it is worth investigating as your required beginning date comes onto your radar screen—hopefully, a year in advance.

In the third year, the process of figuring required withdrawals gets easier. You'll divide your account balance by your life expectancy as long as you have money in your account. If you only withdraw the required amount each year, the table is designed to keep your savings alive until you are 115. (No promise that it can do the same for you.)

Of course, you can always take out more than the required distribution amount. The IRS will not complain about that because the government will be getting tax dollars that it would otherwise have had to wait for. But you can't count any additional amount against a required amount for another year.

HELP IS ON THE WAY

NOW THAT YOU KNOW HOW to figure your required minimum distribution, I have news for you: I feel a little bit like the math teacher who has forced her students to tackle long division on their own and then produced a stash of hand-held calculators. The new IRS rules include a proposal to require the custodians of your IRA accounts to calculate the minimum withdrawal amounts for their customers and report them both to the account owners and the IRS. This measure is still a work in progress. As a first step, IRA custodians will be required to notify current account holders that a required minimum distribution is due and either calculate the amount or offer to calculate it for them. (The focus here is on IRAs because by age 70½, most retirement savings have found their way to an IRA because workplace plan rules typically require that you get your money out of your employer's plans by age 65, unless you're still working.) Beginning in 2004, custodians will have to report to the IRS accounts that are subject to required minimum distributions, but the current rules stop short of requiring them to report the amounts.

However, I think the IRS is going to prevail. In fact, I think it is a key trade-off for the simplification that the IRS offered in its new rules. Now, certainly there was evidence that the number of people affected by these complex rules was increasing every year. And perhaps the IRS saw the headaches mounting. Or, perhaps it saw its own headaches mounting, as the number of requests for private letter rulings have turned sharply upward. (Private letter rulings are requests that come from individuals who want the IRS to take special consideration of their circumstances.)

But those reasons aside, the key motivation of the IRS was in all likelihood financial. With an estimated $4 trillion invested in retirement accounts, most of which is likely to find its way into IRAs, no doubt the IRS wants to make sure it gets the tax dollars it is due. Until now, there has been no effective way for the IRS to determine whether an individual was taking adequate distributions after age 70½—or indeed, any distributions at all. Unless you came under the scrutiny of the IRS for another reason, or you were picked for a random audit, there was simply no way for the government to know that you were skipping out on withdrawals and letting your accounts fatten with the benefit of tax-deferred compounding.

If that changes, and IRA custodians are required to figure an individual's required minimum distribution, you'll be off the hook. Yet, it's still a good idea to know the underlying formula. It will remain in your best interest to check the accuracy of your custodians' calculations.

MINIMUM DISTRIBUTIONS FROM MULTIPLE ACCOUNTS

IF YOU HAVE more than one traditional, SEP, or rollover IRA, you can aggregate the balances to determine the amount of your required minimum distribution. Then, you can take the money out of just one IRA or more than

REQUIRED MINIMUM DISTRIBUTIONS GENERAL RULES

REQUIRED BEGINNING DATE	EXCEPTION
April 1 of the year after you turn 70½	◆ you are still working and you don't own 5 percent of the company ◆ you have a pre-1987 balance in a 403(b) ◆ Roth IRAs

TABLE USED TO CALCULATE DISTRIBUTION AMOUNT	EXCEPTION
Uniform Lifetime Table (Table A)	◆ your spouse is your sole beneficiary and 10+ years younger than you are. Use the Joint Life and Last Survivor Expectancy Table (Table B).

one. It's your call. There is, however, a significant tax wrinkle that applies to figuring taxes on your withdrawals from multiple IRAs if you have both tax-deductible IRAs and IRAs that were funded with **AFTER-TAX DOLLARS**. (For more information, see Number 11.)

You can use the same aggregation strategy if you have more than one workplace tax-deferred annuity—not an individual tax-deferred annuity that you can fund with after-tax dollars above and beyond your workplace or IRA limits.

However, if you have more than one 401(k) or **PROFIT SHARING PLAN** or some other type of qualified plan, you'll have to compute a minimum distribution amount for each one and take the amount out of each one. Another argument for consolidation and rolling over to an IRA or an annuity.

SPEAKING OF ANNUITIES

IF YOU RECEIVE SOME or all of your retirement plan benefits in the form of an annuity, or if you roll your retirement plan over into an annuity, the income payments you receive

TABLE A: UNIFORM LIFETIME TABLE

AGE OF IRA OWNER OR PLAN PARTICIPANT	APPLICABLE DISTRIBUTION PERIOD (LIFE EXPECTANCY DIVISOR)	AGE OF IRA OWNER OR PLAN PARTICIPANT	APPLICABLE DISTRIBUTION PERIOD (LIFE EXPECTANCY DIVISOR)
70	27.4	93	9.6
71	26.5	94	9.1
72	25.6	95	8.6
73	24.7	96	8.1
74	23.8	97	7.6
75	22.9	98	7.1
76	22.0	99	6.7
77	21.2	100	6.3
78	20.3	101	5.9
79	19.5	102	5.5
80	18.7	103	5.2
81	17.9	104	4.9
82	17.1	105	4.5
83	16.3	106	4.2
84	15.5	107	3.9
85	14.8	108	3.7
86	14.1	109	3.4
87	13.4	110	3.1
88	12.7	111	2.9
89	12.0	112	2.6
90	11.4	113	2.4
91	10.8	114	2.1
92	10.2	115+	1.9

SOURCE: INTERNAL REVENUE SERVICE, JUNE 2002

must satisfy your required minimum distributions. The good news is that annuity companies understand these requirements and are accustomed to structuring annuities with required distributions in mind. But you'll have to make sure that you choose the right type of annuity in order to pass IRS scrutiny. Here's what the IRS will expect:
◆ that your annuity payments are made at least once a year.

TABLE B: JOINT LIFE AND LAST SURVIVOR EXPECTANCY TABLE (FOR OWNERS WITH SPOUSES MORE THAN 10 YEARS YOUNGER)

SPOUSAL BENEFICIARY AGE	YOUR PRESENT AGE						
	70	71	72	73	74	75	76
50	35.1	35.0	34.9	34.8	34.8	34.7	34.6
51	34.3	34.2	34.1	34.0	33.9	33.8	33.8
52	33.4	33.3	33.2	33.1	33.0	33.0	32.9
53	32.6	32.5	32.4	32.3	32.2	32.1	32.0
54	31.8	31.7	31.6	31.5	31.4	31.3	31.2
55	31.1	30.9	30.8	30.6	30.5	30.4	30.3
56	30.3	30.1	30.0	29.8	29.7	29.6	29.5
57	29.5	29.4	29.2	29.1	28.9	28.8	28.7
58	28.8	28.6	28.4	28.3	28.1	28.0	27.9
59	28.1	27.9	27.7	27.5	27.4	27.2	27.1
60		27.2	27.0	26.8	26.6	26.5	26.3
61			26.3	26.1	25.9	25.7	25.6
62				25.4	25.2	25.0	24.8
63					24.5	24.3	24.1
64						23.6	23.4
65							22.7
66							
67							
68							
69							
70							
71							
72							
73							
74							

SOURCE: INTERNAL REVENUE SERVICE

◆ that you choose either a **LIFE ANNUITY** or a **TERM CERTAIN ANNUITY**.

If you choose a life annuity, it must indeed cover your entire lifetime or your lifetime in combination with that of a beneficiary who may or may not be your spouse. If you

YOUR PRESENT AGE

77	78	79	80	81	82	83	84	85
34.6	34.5	34.5	34.5	34.4	34.4	34.4	34.3	34.3
33.7	33.6	33.6	33.6	33.5	33.5	33.5	33.4	33.4
32.8	32.8	32.7	32.7	32.6	32.6	32.6	32.5	32.5
32.0	31.9	31.8	31.8	31.8	31.7	31.7	31.7	31.6
31.1	31.0	31.0	30.9	30.9	30.8	30.8	30.8	30.7
30.3	30.2	30.1	30.1	30.0	30.0	29.9	29.9	29.9
29.4	29.3	29.3	29.2	29.2	29.1	29.1	29.0	29.0
28.6	28.5	28.4	28.4	28.3	28.3	28.2	28.2	28.1
27.8	27.7	27.6	27.5	27.5	27.4	27.4	27.3	27.3
27.0	26.9	26.8	26.7	26.6	26.6	26.5	26.5	26.4
26.2	26.1	26.0	25.9	25.8	25.8	25.7	25.6	25.6
25.4	25.3	25.2	25.1	25.0	24.9	24.9	24.8	24.8
24.7	24.6	24.4	24.3	24.2	24.1	24.1	24.0	23.9
23.9	23.8	23.7	23.6	23.4	23.4	23.3	23.2	23.1
23.2	23.1	22.9	22.8	22.7	22.6	22.5	22.4	22.3
22.5	22.4	22.2	22.1	21.9	21.8	21.7	21.6	21.6
21.8	21.7	21.5	21.3	21.2	21.1	21.0	20.9	20.8
	21.0	20.8	20.6	20.5	20.4	20.2	20.1	20.1
		20.1	20.0	19.8	19.7	19.5	19.4	19.3
			19.3	19.1	19.0	18.8	18.7	18.6
				18.5	18.3	18.2	18.0	17.9
					17.7	17.5	17.4	17.3
						16.9	16.7	16.6
							16.1	16.0
								15.4

choose a term certain annuity, the term has to be long enough to be in keeping with the life expectancy that you would use to figure your own required minimum distribution. You can't change the term once you begin to receive payments. And generally, the payments must be level, although an exception is made if you are entitled to a cost-of-living adjustment or investment gains in your portfolio, which could occur if you choose a **VARIABLE ANNUITY**.

Just as with other types of retirement plans and accounts, your first annuity payment must come on or before your required beginning date, which is usually April 1 after the year you turn 70½, but it could be later if one of the exceptions mentioned above applies.

REQUIRED DISTRIBUTIONS WHEN YOU ARE DIVORCED OR SEPARATED

IF YOU ARE REQUIRED to share your workplace retirement savings with a spouse, an ex-spouse, or your child because a court order has mandated it, the required minimum distribution rules apply to both parties' interests in your account. Your age determines the required beginning date and you will be responsible for paying any penalty that is incurred because of a missed or insufficient required withdrawal. You'll also be responsible for paying the income tax on the distribution if the other party is someone other than your spouse.

If the court order requires and your plan allows you to set up a separate account for the other party entitled to share in your savings, you have one more option for settling on a life expectancy. You can use the one based on your age; you can use the joint life expectancy of you and the other party if that person is your ex-spouse and is more than ten years younger than you; or you can use the other party's single-life expectancy. The decision is yours, although a savvy attorney is likely to nail this option down as part of the court order.

PENALTY BOX

WHAT'S AT STAKE for missing a required distribution or taking an insufficient distribution? A lot. The IRS has reserved one of the stiffest penalties of all for individuals who fail to take timely and adequate required minimum distributions—50 percent of that required amount! Plus,

you'll be required to take the entire amount of the distribution. What's more, if there is a pattern of ignoring your
required minimum distributions, the IRS can disqualify
your plan or account, and force you to take all the money
out at once and pay taxes on it. This is not a pleasant
thought. If you have overlooked or misunderstood the
rules on required minimum distributions, you should talk
with a tax professional and get on the right side of the IRS
as soon as possible. Of course, if financial companies begin
reporting these amounts to both account holders and the
IRS, it should reduce the incidence of error—uninten-
tional or otherwise.

Minimizing Taxes and Avoiding Penalties

Minimizing Taxes

Your decisions about withdrawals—how much you take, when you take it, and from what accounts— affect your taxes.

TAXES ARE LIKE a silent, hungry gorilla lurking inside your retirement savings. You may feel good about how much you have put away over the years, but remember: No matter when you take the money out, approximately one out of every three or four dollars will go to feed the gorilla.

Yet, you can have an amazing amount of control over your tax bill if you adjust your thinking to focus not on the taxes you'll pay, but on the income you can generate if you are tax-wise about your withdrawals. Although the tax gorilla will claim its share each time you take money out of your accounts, there are ways to keep your taxes as low as possible and special opportunities that apply to some accounts. How you take your withdrawals and your age can also be deciding factors in the amount of tax you'll owe on withdrawals—or when you will owe it.

GENERAL TAX RULES

◆ **When you take money out of your tax-advantaged retirement savings accounts, you'll owe tax on your withdrawals.** When the money is yours, it's taxed in the same year. You deferred paying those taxes when you saved. Now it's time to pay up.

◆ **Most withdrawals are taxed as ordinary income.** If you're in a lower income tax bracket when you take money out of your accounts, that's a very good deal. You were in a higher bracket when you earned it, but you won't have to make up the difference. And if you're in a higher tax bracket when you withdraw it, you must be some kind of investment whiz. Either way, you're ahead.

◆ **You may owe an additional "penalty" tax if you withdraw money from your tax-advantaged accounts before 59½ — or if you fail to withdraw a minimum amount after age 70½.** There are plenty of exceptions to this rule, which are covered in Number 9. In general, you want to avoid penalties, because they reduce both your current and future income—money lost to penalties is lost to future tax-deferred compounding.

◆ **If you weren't entitled to a tax deduction for your retirement savings contribution, you won't be taxed on the full amount of your withdrawal.** Some retirement accounts accept **AFTER-TAX DOLLARS**. Nondeductible traditional IRAs fit into this category. So do certain company-sponsored retirement savings plans—a thrift plan, for example, or an **EMPLOYEE STOCK OWNERSHIP PLAN (ESOP)** —that allow you to sock away a little more even if you've maxed out on the limits to another plan. **TAX-DEFERRED ANNUITIES** that you purchase on your own are also acquired with after-tax dollars. The money in these accounts grows **TAX DEFERRED**, so only the earnings on your account are taxable when you make a withdrawal.

If you have a nondeductible traditional IRA, there's a special tax form you'll be required to file each time you make a withdrawal from it—IRS Form 8606. And there's a tax formula that you'll follow to compute the amount that is taxable.

If you have both deductible and nondeductible IRAs, you'll aggregate their combined value to compute the tax on any IRA withdrawal. An example makes this easier to understand:

You have a SEP IRA worth $100,000, which you accumulated through regular contributions that you were allowed to claim as an income tax deduction each year. You also have a traditional IRA worth $50,000. (Every year for ten years you made a $2,000 nondeductible contribution to an IRA, and now it is worth $50,000.) During your first year of retirement, you withdrew $5,000 from your SEP IRA. How much of your withdrawal is taxable?

STEP 1 Add the fair market value of your account to the amount of your **DISTRIBUTION**:

$100,000 + $50,000 + $5,000 = $155,000

STEP 2 Divide the amount of your nondeductible contributions by the amount from step 1:

$50,000 ÷ $155,000 = 0.323

STEP 3 Multiply the amount from step 2 by the amount of your distribution to find the portion of your distribution that is not taxable:

0.323 x $5,000 = $1,615

When you figure your income tax, you'll report a taxable withdrawal of $3,385. You'll repeat the calculation each year that there is money remaining in your IRAs. Because this paperwork can become onerous, you may want to consider drawing down the balance of your nondeductible IRAs first. Although you figure taxes on the aggregated amount, you can take the withdrawal out of any account you choose—or from more than one account.

What if you don't remember the amount of your original nondeductible contributions, which is also known as the **COST BASIS** for the account—a tax term for its ground zero starting value? Your account custodian can figure it out and in fact may report it to you on your account statement as a matter of course.

After-tax money in a workplace retirement savings account works differently. Under **OLD IRS RULES**, you were virtually guaranteed to take a sizable tax hit when you made any withdrawal from these accounts. You couldn't roll these after-tax contributions to another plan. Once they moved to you, taxes were due. Also—and this is still true—if you decided to **ROLL OVER** your 401(k) or other accounts that had been funded with pretax dollars, your employer would probably require that you liquidate *all* your accounts. Employers do what they have to do to let you keep your money in your retirement savings accounts—up to a point. But given the opportunity, they would just as soon have you take your money someplace else. You are a cost to them as long as you remain on their books.

The good news is that the 2001 tax law loosened the rules on after-tax savings. Now, you can roll it over into an IRA or another qualified plan and keep the money growing tax deferred until you withdraw it. There's one condition: The new plan or custodian has to be both willing and equipped to account for these after-tax contributions *separately* so that when you do take the money out, it will be clear what money was never taxed and what money was taxed. That's more likely if you roll it over to an IRA than if you try to move it to another plan. (Remember, just because the IRS or Congress allow it, doesn't mean a plan has to do it.) When it comes time to take money out of that account, the IRS will assume that you are withdrawing a pro rata amount from both pools—the pretax and the after-tax savings.

You may also have the option of turning your after-tax savings into an annuity. Annuity payments make taxes easy. A portion of every payment is assumed to be a pro rata amount of your original contribution, and that amount is not taxable.

Tax-deferred annuities purchased with after-tax dollars work the same. A portion of every annuity payment you receive is assumed to be a pro rata amount of your original contribution. (With an annuity, a contribution is actually a "payment." Don't confuse the "payments" you make with the payment you receive.) The insurance company from which you purchased the annuity will take care of the tax calculation and tax reporting you need each year.

And the fabulous Roth IRA? Withdrawals from a Roth IRA generally are tax free. You can always withdraw the money you contributed and owe no tax once your account is five years old and you're 59½ *or* you turn your savings into a stream of income based on your life expectancy. You can also withdraw your Roth IRA earnings free of federal income tax. You may owe state income tax on Roth IRA withdrawals. States vary in their treatment.

◆ **Generally speaking, you can't claim investment losses against taxes due on your retirement withdrawals.** The money you withdraw will be taxed without respect to your investment success over the years. If your account was worth $200,000 at its peak, in 2000, after years of contributions and gains, and only $150,000 in 2003, there are no sympathetic ears at the IRS. After all, your losses are also likely to be their losses. Remember, they never collected their income tax dollars from you along the way.

There is one exception: If you contribute after-tax dollars and the amount you withdraw is actually lower than the amount you contributed, you may claim a loss. For example, say that you contributed $2,000 to a non-deductible IRA in 2000 and because it was invested in an Internet fund, it quickly sank to $800. Two years later, when you retire, it is worth $700. You liquidate the account and claim a loss of $1,300 on your income tax.

◆ **Taxes will be withheld before you receive a check for any withdrawal over $200 from your IRA or workplace retirement savings plan.** Your workplace savings plan is required by law to withhold 20 percent of any withdrawal over $200. Your IRA custodian will withhold 10 percent. This may be more—or less—than you will actually owe at tax time, but the standard amount is not negotiable.

◆ **You have approximately sixty days to change your mind about a withdrawal, but it may not be easy to wipe the slate clean.** Here's what that means. Say you want to start a new business when you leave your employer at age 65 and you decide to cash in your $50,000 401(k). By law your employer will withhold 20 percent, or $10,000, and you'll receive a check for $40,000.

Then, let's say you have second thoughts about your plans. You realize you will need more than $40,000, and you could probably take a second mortgage on your house for $100,000 if you needed to. You'll have sixty days to roll your retirement savings into an IRA and rescue the tax advantages for your retirement money.

Just one small problem. You withdrew $50,000 but now you only have $40,000. If you have the additional $10,000 to restore the account to its original value, it's a good idea to do so. If you only put $40,000 back into the account, the $10,000 that went to the IRS will be treated as a withdrawal. You'll owe taxes on it—which, in a sense, you've already overpaid—and depending on your total tax picture, the IRS may owe you money in the end. A hollow victory.

EXCEPTIONS AND OPPORTUNITIES

THOSE SEVEN RULES apply to *most* every individual and *most* common retirement savings plans. But there are also some important exceptions, as well as some valuable opportunities to do better than the general rules allow— or at least to take an alternate view of your tax situation before you start writing checks to the IRS.

The first two apply to individuals who were born before 1936 and **GRANDFATHERED** under tax laws that preceded the landmark retirement legislation of 1974.

A SPECIAL TAX FORMULA MAY BE AVAILABLE IF YOU WITHDRAW ALL OF YOUR RETIREMENT SAVINGS AT ONCE

IT'S IMPORTANT TO understand that this is rarely a good strategy. The long-term potential for tax-deferred growth is a very big deal. Your $100,000 invested over fifteen years at 8 percent is worth about twice as much in a tax-deferred account than it would be in a taxable account. Even after taxes are paid, most workers would be tens of thousands of dollars to the good. The opportunity to continue accumulating tax-deferred earnings on your accounts well into retirement is not to be taken lightly. Tax deferral is a very powerful tool. But if you are determined to take all of your money at once, you may be able to save some on taxes if you follow the prescribed rules for a **LUMP SUM DISTRIBUTION**. Here's what that means: You must take all of the money in all like accounts. For example, profit-sharing and 401(k) accounts fall into the same IRS category. Likewise for money purchase and **DEFINED BENEFIT PLANS**. If you take all the money from one, you must also liquidate the other plan in order for your withdrawal to qualify as a lump sum distribution. And you must take it all in one calendar year.

ELIGIBILITY FOR TEN-YEAR FORWARD AVERAGING

YOU'RE ELIGIBLE TO USE a special tax approach called **TEN-YEAR FORWARD AVERAGING** if you were born before 1936; if you have not used the formula on withdrawals you've made from qualified retirement savings plans since 1986; and if you've been a plan participant for at least five years. Ten-year averaging applies only to qualified workplace retirement savings plans. You can use it on your company's 401(k) and profit-sharing plans, as well as a Keogh, but not on a 403(b) or an IRA.

◆ **Strict rules govern your withdrawal:** Even if you are eligible to use ten-year averaging, you must follow precise IRS rules when you withdraw your money. You must take all of the money in your account—and all in the same tax year. A partial distribution won't qualify, and you can't take some of the money in December and the balance in January.

◆ **How ten-year averaging works:** Your tax bill is figured as if you had stretched your withdrawal over a ten-year period, although your tax payment will be due in the year of your withdrawal. For the tax calculation, you'll be treated as single, even if you are married. And if your withdrawal is less than $70,000, the IRS will give you an additional break called a **MINIMUM DISTRIBUTION ALLOWANCE**.

There's a lot of calculating involved with the use of ten-year averaging. It's not hard to do, but it is exacting. You'll use IRS Form 4972 to determine your minimum distribution allowance, if you are entitled to it, and then you'll compute your income tax using the 1986 individual rates (see the table on page 123). Or, you'll call your accountant—not a bad choice on this one.

Is it worth it? The answer generally depends on the size of your withdrawal and your future tax status.

◆ If you absolutely need the money and you are eligible, it could save you a substantial sum of money. Using ten-year averaging, your tax bill could be just under $6,000 for a $50,000 withdrawal compared to $17,500 if you paid federal income tax in the 35 percent bracket.

◆ On small withdrawals, the opportunity to use the minimum distribution allowance is a pretty good deal.

◆ If you expect your tax rate to remain high in retirement, the tax rate you use with ten-year averaging could be attractive. Tax rates for 1986 were lower at the low end of the income scale and higher at the high end of the income scale than they were after the tax law changes of 2001.

You may be able to treat some portion of your withdrawals as **CAPITAL GAINS**, which are currently taxed at only 20 percent.

Like ten-year averaging, special capital gains treatment is available only to individuals born before 1936 and applies only to individuals who were participating in a workplace retirement savings plan before 1974. What's more, it only applies to withdrawals that can be attributed to those early savings. But you don't have to worry about calculating the amount. Your plan administrator will do it and report it to you. You can use it in combination with ten-year averaging, but you can also use it if you're paying ordinary income tax on the rest of your withdrawal.

IF YOU OWN EMPLOYER STOCK IN YOUR RETIREMENT SAVINGS PLAN ...

YOU'RE ENTITLED TO pay capital gains tax on the appreciation over and above your purchase price—if you take the stock **IN KIND** from your account. You can use this special tax treatment of the **NET UNREALIZED APPRECIATION** of your stock in combination with ten-year averaging, if you're eligible. Or you can simply hold onto the stock and pay ordinary income tax on all but the net unrealized appreciation, which would be subject to capital gains tax when you sold it.

As with other special tax treatments, it's very important to follow IRS rules in order to qualify for this opportunity to use the capital gains tax rate—which is a favorable 20 percent in 2003—on a portion of your retirement savings withdrawal. It's only available if you withdraw the stock itself—you can't sell it and withdraw the cash, although you can sell it after you make the withdrawal from your account. And you lose the opportunity to use this approach if you roll the stock over into an IRA or another employer's qualified plan. Deciding whether the special tax treatment is more valuable than the future tax-deferred growth, which you will give up, may require some professional tax guidance. For more detailed information on how to take advantage of this approach and when it applies, see Number 21.

If you receive payment from your spouse's workplace retirement savings plan under a court-approved order as part of a divorce or separation settlement, you are entitled to any special treatment that is available to your spouse.

If you and your spouse have agreed that you should receive a portion of his or her qualified retirement plan, you can preserve its tax benefits by rolling the money over to your own qualified plan or IRA. But this can only happen if a **QUALIFIED DOMESTIC RELATIONS ORDER or QDRO** has been drawn up and approved by a court of law. If your spouse is eligible for ten-year averaging, you're eligible to use it if, instead of a rollover, you choose to take the pay-

IRS FORMS FOR REPORTING RETIREMENT DISTRIBUTIONS AND OTHER ACTIVITIES

FORM	USE THIS FORM TO REPORT THE FOLLOWING RETIREMENT-RELATED DISTRIBUTIONS, CONTRIBUTIONS, CONVERSIONS, AND RECHARACTERIZATIONS
4972	**Tax on Lump-Sum Distributions**

Answer the questions in part I to determine whether you must file this form. You'll need information from your Form 1099-R, which reports the amount of your distribution. There's a section to elect the 20 percent capital gains treatment, if you qualify; a section to elect 10-year averaging; and a worksheet to calculate net unrealized appreciation in employer securities, if you elect to include it in your taxable income, as well as your minimum distribution allowance.

5329 **Additional taxes on qualified plans (including IRAs) and other tax-favored accounts**

A distribution *or* contribution that is subject to a penalty tax, including:

◆ distributions from an IRA or a qualified retirement plan before age 59 1/2

◆ distributions that meet the exception to the early withdrawal penalty tax but are not properly coded in box 7 of Form 1099-R

◆ required minimum distributions you failed to take from your tax-advantaged accounts

◆ contributions to IRAs in excess of eligible amounts received before age 59 1/2 from an IRA or from a qualified retirement plan

5330 **Return of Excise Taxes Related to Employee Benefit Plans**

◆ an excess contribution to a 403(b) plan

◆ a disqualified contribution to a qualified plan

◆ certain dispositions from an ESOP

Many of the situations reported on Form 5330 apply to employers and not to employees.

8606 **Nondeductible IRAs and Coverdell ESAs**

◆ nondeductible contributions to and distributions from traditional, SEP, and SIMPLE IRAs

◆ conversions and partial conversions of IRAs to Roth IRAs

◆ recharacterizations of Roth IRAs back to an IRA

◆ distributions from Roth IRAs

FEDERAL INCOME TAX RATE SCHEDULE FOR THE 10-YEAR AVERAGING TAX OPTION (1986 TAX RATES*)

IF ONE-TENTH OF THE LUMP-SUM DISTRIBUTION IS:		THEN ONE-TENTH** OF THE TAX IS:	
OVER	BUT NOT OVER		OF THE AMOUNT OVER
$0	$1,190	——— 11%	$0
$1,190	$2,270	$130.90 + 12%	$1,190
$2,270	$4,530	$260.50 + 14%	$2,270
$4,530	$6,690	$576.90 + 15%	$4,530
$6,690	$9,170	$900.90 + 16%	$6,690
$9,170	$11,440	$1,297.70 + 18%	$9,170
$11,440	$13,710	$1,706.30 + 20%	$11,440
$13,710	$17,160	$2,160.30 + 23%	$13,710
$17,160	$22,880	$2,953.80 + 26%	$17,160
$22,880	$28,600	$4,441.00 + 30%	$22,880
$28,600	$34,320	$6,157.00 + 34%	$28,600
$34,320	$42,300	$8,101.80 + 38%	$34,320
$42,300	$57,190	$11,134.20 + 42%	$42,300
$57,190	$85,790	$17,388.00 + 48%	$57,190
$85,790	———	$31,116.00 + 50%	$85,790

* Tax rates are for single taxpayers. But you must use this table regardless of your marital status.
** The result is multiplied by 10 to arrive at the tax using 10-year averaging

ment as a lump sum distribution. However, averaging is the only special treatment available. No special capital gains treatment is available for money that was accumulated prior to 1974 or for employer stock with net unrealized appreciation that becomes yours as part of the QDRO. If you decide to take some or all of the money and put it to use prior to retirement, you'll owe ordinary income tax on your withdrawal. But you won't be subject an early withdrawal penalty tax.

Most payments from a retirement plan to satisfy the terms of a QDRO go to a spouse. However, if the money goes to someone else—a child, for example—the account owner is the one who takes the hit in terms of taxes. If he or she is eligible to use ten-year averaging, it's available. Mercifully, no early withdrawal penalty tax is due.

The special rules affecting **TRANSFERS** of money from one party to another in a divorce apply only to qualified plans and qualified annuities. They do not apply to IRAs, for example. And they do not apply if the agreement has not been formalized by a QDRO.

A couple of other wrinkles to be aware of: Although a transfer of retirement plan assets under a QDRO gets the blessing of the courts and the IRS, your plan may not allow it. And plan rules take precedence. For example, your plan may not allow any distribution whatsoever until you reach retirement age as specified in the plan. Before you proceed too far into your legal proceedings, it's a good idea to ask about any restrictions that could affect the final outcome of your agreement.

Penalties—and How to Avoid Them

You can always get at your retirement savings penalty free, if you know the ropes.

PENALTIES THAT APPLY to your retirement savings accounts are like the double yellow lines down the middle of the interstate. They are meant to keep you on the correct side of the road, whether you are coming or going. And every once in a while there's a little space where you can cross the line without breaking the law.

There are two types of penalties that can be levied against your retirement savings account: those that apply to the money you put into your accounts—your contributions; and those that apply to the money you take out (or should have taken out of your accounts, but didn't).

PENALTIES THAT APPLY TO CONTRIBUTIONS

ANY EXCESS CONTRIBUTION to your retirement savings plans, regardless of circumstances, is subject to penalty tax: 6 percent for excess contributions to an IRA and 10 percent for excess contributions to a qualified retirement plan. What's more, you'll owe this penalty every year that the excess contribution remains in your account.

What is an excess contribution? Any amount that is higher than the limits set by Congress for all types of retirement plans. Here's an example:

Say you took advantage of the new limits that were introduced in 2002 to allow you to put up to $3,500 a year in an IRA after age 50. Early in 2003, you make your $3,500 contribution. Then you suddenly decide to retire soon after that and your total income for 2003 is only $2,000. Now you have an excess contribution of $1,500 in your IRA. If you catch it before you file your 2003 taxes, you can take the money out and you're off the hook. However, let's say it just slips your mind. But it is discovered in 2005 by your accountant in a routine review of your finances. You'll owe a 6 percent penalty for 2003, 2004, and 2005. It only amounts to $270, plus 6 percent on any earnings that can be attributed to the additional $1,500 contribution, but what a nasty surprise!

I asked CPA Norman Posner, with Samet & Company of Chestnut Hill, Massachusetts, why not just ignore the slip-up in hope that the IRS will do the same? It's not worth it, says Posner. Although the IRS has not had an effective mechanism in place to catch the occasional indiscretion, it is getting better. If your error is small, so is the penalty. File Form 5329, which is required to report an overcontribution, take the money—and any earnings that can be attributed to it—out of the account, and be done with it, says Posner. Why risk getting caught by the IRS over something small? And if the error is substantial, there's too much at stake not to correct it. For example, a small business owner who consistently over-contributes for himself runs the risk of disqualifying the entire retirement plan for all the employees, a risk that certainly isn't worth taking.

Most excess contributions are made to IRAs or to small business retirement plans when the business owner incorrectly calculates the contributions. Your workplace retirement savings plan usually keeps contributions in line because it is programmed to catch any error. But there is one way that plans can go wrong: with an ineligible rollover.

Say you retire at age 71 and you direct your plan's trustee to **ROLL OVER** your retirement plan balance to an IRA. Because of your age, you will be required to take a **REQUIRED MINIMUM DISTRIBUTION** during the year. As a result, your plan should deduct that amount from your account balance and distribute it directly to you before the account is rolled over. Even if they don't, you must report it as income. And you must remove the amount from your rollover IRA or it will be considered an excess contribution and subject to a 6 percent annual penalty for as long as it remains in your account.

PENALTIES THAT APPLY
TO WITHDRAWALS

ONCE YOU BEGIN THE COUNTDOWN to your retirement years, you're less likely to find yourself in the penalty box for an excess contribution than for a missed or prohibited withdrawal. Withdrawal penalties fall into three categories:

◆ a 10 percent penalty tax on money withdrawn too early

◆ a 50 percent penalty tax on money that is *not* withdrawn in accordance with the IRS rules on required minimum distributions, which kick in when you are 70½

◆ yikes—a penalty of up to 100 percent on a prohibited withdrawal in the form of a loan from a Keogh plan.

EARLY WITHDRAWALS

STRICTLY SPEAKING, money withdrawn before age 59½ from your workplace retirement savings plan or your IRA is subject to a 10 percent penalty tax. But there are a host of exceptions (see the box on the following page). An exception is made by qualified workplace savings plans if you are 55 and you have lost your job. Also, dividends received from employer stock that you own in an **EMPLOYER STOCK OWNERSHIP PLAN**, or **ESOP**, escape the early withdrawal penalty. You can also avoid the penalty tax on money you withdraw from your qualified workplace retirement savings plan:

◆ if you are disabled

◆ if you need money to pay medical expenses

◆ to meet obligations that are part of a **QUALIFIED DOMESTIC RELATIONS ORDER (QDRO)**

◆ and, of course, if you die.

EXCEPTIONS TO 10 PERCENT EARLY WITHDRAWAL PENALTY TAX

IRAS

1. Permanent disability
2. Death—money taken by your beneficiary is penalty free
3. Unreimbursed medical expenses that exceed 7½% of adjusted gross income (AGI)
4. Substantially equal periodic payments following one of three IRS-approved formulas
5. Payment of medical insurance premiums after 12 weeks of unemployment compensation; presumed eligibility for unemployment for self-employed
6. First-time home purchase (subject to lifetime limit of $10,000)
7. Qualified higher education expenses IRA owner and/or eligible family members
8. Forced distribution because IRS has taken funds to pay back taxes
9. Withdrawal to correct an overcontribution

401(K)S AND OTHER QUALIFIED PLANS

1. Permanent disability
2. Death—money taken by your beneficiary is penalty free.
3. Unreimbursed medical expenses exceed 7½% of adjusted gross income (AGI).
4. Substantially equal periodic payments following one of three IRS-approved formulas
5. A Qualified Domestic Relations Order (QDRO) mandates a distribution from your account to a former spouse, child, or dependent
6. Separation from employment at age 55 or older
7. Dividends from employer stock that you own in an Employer Stock Ownership Plan (ESOP)
8. Withdrawal to correct an overcontribution

Withdrawing money for medical expenses is a bit tricky—and you won't be able to escape the penalty on the full amount of your withdrawal. The penalty break only applies to the portion of your medical expenses that would be deductible if you itemized deductions on your tax return. But you can get the break even if you *don't* itemize your deductions.

IRAs also offer exceptions to the penalty tax, which include a few that are not allowed by workplace plans. For example, you can take money out of your IRAs to cover higher education expenses and to make a first-time home purchase. (These are considered "hardship withdrawals" by a workplace savings plan and would be penalized.) You can also withdraw money to pay your health insurance premiums if you are unemployed or were recently unemployed. But you must have received unemployment compensation—or have been eligible for unemployment if you are self-employed—and the window of opportunity for exercising this option begins twelve weeks after you've begun receiving unemployment and ends sixty days after you go back to work. The conditions you must meet are constraining, and you should square away the details with your tax adviser.

Roth IRAs are different from rollover and traditional contributory IRAs, including SEP and SIMPLE IRAs. Because there's no up-front tax break for the contributions you make to a Roth IRA, you can withdraw your contribution at any time and avoid the 10 percent early withdrawal penalty tax. However, if you withdraw an amount that exceeds your contributions (i.e., you're now tapping your account's earnings), the excess will be subject to the penalty tax unless the account has been in place for five years and you are 59½, or unless you can avail yourself of one of the exceptions that apply, the same that apply to other IRAs.

An extra-harsh penalty applies to early withdrawals from a SIMPLE IRA: If you take money out of your account for any reason that is not included in the list of exceptions to the early penalty tax during the first two years you participate, you'll owe a whopping 25 percent penalty on your withdrawal. After two years, the penalty falls back to 10 percent, in line with other types of IRAs.

Two final exceptions to the early withdrawal penalty tax: if you take money out of your account to correct an excess contribution, or if the feds come in and take your assets because you owe back taxes. Gee, thanks.

You should never take money out of your tax-advantaged retirement savings plans and pay a penalty, however, until you have considered your options for taking the money penalty free, even if you don't qualify for one of the exceptions listed above. If you are 25 and you cash in your 401(k) to splurge on a $3,000 vacation, there's not much anyone can do to get you off the hook: You'll pay income tax plus a 10 percent penalty, all of which whittles away at your prospects for a sound retirement.

But, let's say you find yourself out of work and down on your luck for an extended period of time. You're 52, and you'd really like to use some of your IRA savings, which amounts to $50,000, to keep yourself afloat while you continue to look for work. The IRS says that it will skip the penalty if you turn your savings into a stream of income based on one of three sanctioned formulas. (For more detailed information, see Number 20.) The catch, however, is that you cannot take more than your calculated amount. You can't change the formula from year to year, even if you no longer need the money. And you must keep the payments up for at least five years or until you turn 59½, whichever is longer.

There's a fair amount of wisdom built into this practice. On one hand, the IRS is willing to give workers early access to some portion of their retirement savings penalty free. But it has also made restrictions tight enough so that it would be unattractive to take this course unless you really needed to.

You can use this approach to take money out of any tax-advantaged retirement savings plan, but practically speaking, it's easier to do when your money is in an IRA. If you try to do it with money left in your workplace retirement savings plan, you are unlikely to have much flexibility in how the withdrawals are computed. In fact, your employer's formula for computing the monthly or annual income may not follow IRS guidelines. And once you begin a **SYSTEMATIC WITHDRAWAL PLAN**, you may find yourself locked in. Do yourself a favor and roll the money into an IRA so that you can be in charge.

LATE WITHDRAWALS

ANYONE WHO THINKS OF an IRA, Keogh, or workplace retirement savings as a private cache of funds, to be dipped into at will, has another thought coming. Congress laid down the law about how much you can put into these accounts and how often. The IRS tells you how much you must take out and when. If you fail to follow the rules on **REQUIRED MINIMUM DISTRIBUTIONS** you'll face the stiffest penalty of all—50 percent of the amount you were scheduled to withdraw. Plus, you'll have to take the money you were required to distribute for the year. So if you were required to withdraw $10,000 from your IRA, and you failed to do it, you'll owe a penalty tax of $5,000, plus you'll have to make the $10,000 withdrawal. All told, your account balance is lower by $15,000, plus the income tax you'll owe on the $10,000 withdrawal. For a complete discussion of required minimum distributions, see Number 10.

PROHIBITED WITHDRAWAL

THE IRS MUST HAVE BEEN having a really bad day when it set down the rules for Keogh plans. These qualified plans, which have been around for more than forty years, have one insidious quirk. They allow you to borrow from your account, following the same rules that govern other qualified plans, *unless* you are one of the company's owners. If you break this rule, you could be in for a very stiff penalty. You must report the prohibited transaction on IRS Form 5330 and pay a penalty of 15 percent for every year that the loan remains outstanding. You'll have seven months after year-end to pay the penalty. And if you don't repay the loan, the penalty increases to 100 percent. (I guess they really want you to repay the loan.)

Important Dates and Milestones

The Feds are watching you from age 50 to age 90. Mark these birthdays on a special calendar.

TO YOU, THE MOST IMPORTANT date on your calendar may be the one you've marked for retirement. But the IRS has its own list of important dates. So does the Social Security Administration. Your former employers may also have dates in mind that affect your retirement savings. Some represent obligations. Others represent opportunities. And because some also involve penalties, you want to remain aware of all of them. Here is a list of key birthdays that you should mark on your long-term calendar as you approach your last day on the job.

AGE 50

CONGRATULATIONS, you have already heard from the American Association of Retired Persons (AARP) that you qualify for membership. Social Security may also be interested in your fiftieth birthday: If you're disabled, you are now eligible to collect Social Security retirement benefits earned by a deceased spouse.

AGE 55

IF YOU LOSE YOUR JOB, you are eligible to take money penalty free from your former employer's qualified retirement plan. Practically speaking, the only way you may be able to do this is to take a **LUMP SUM DISTRIBUTION**. If you roll the money over to an IRA or qualified annuity, any money you take out will be subject to a 10 percent early withdrawal penalty. IRAs don't qualify for this special treatment. You may be able to turn it into a stream of systematic withdrawals based on your life expectancy, if this service is offered by the investment manager in charge of your workplace retirement savings plan. Or you can use one of the IRS-approved methods for calculating **SUBSTANTIALLY EQUAL PAYMENTS**. If you take this path, you'll have to keep the income coming for at least five years or until you turn 59½, whichever is longer.

You can take a lump sum distribution penalty free even if you plan on returning to work—even if you go back to work for the same employer. But you can't receive income from the plan of an employer for whom you are currently employed—and you can't return the money to a tax-advantaged plan if it turns out you don't need it.

AGE 59½

GOODBYE PENALTIES! There are no penalties for withdrawals from any employer-sponsored retirement plan, Keogh, or IRA after age 59½. However, if you are still working, your employer is unlikely to let you take money out of your workplace retirement savings plan until you leave.

AGE 60

IF YOU ARE THE SURVIVING SPOUSE of someone who was entitled to Social Security benefits—and you have not remarried—you can begin collecting your deceased spouse's retirement benefits. (The amount you collect won't be 100 percent of what your spouse was entitled to.) But make a note: The age for receiving these benefits gradually increases for persons born after 1939. For example, you'll have to wait until age 67 if you were born in 1962 or later.

AGE 62

THIS IS THE EARLIEST DATE you can begin collecting your own Social Security benefits or benefits you're due through your spouse or former spouse. If you choose to collect Social Security at 62 instead of waiting for your full retirement date, your monthly benefit will be reduced by up to 20 percent.

Age 62 is also the earliest you can obtain a reverse mortgage from the Federal Home Administration. A reverse mortgage lets you turn the equity in your home into a regular stream of income. The AARP offers a good basic overview of reverse mortgages at www.aarp.org/revmort/contents/overview.html. You'll also find help from the National Reverse Mortgage Lenders Association on their website, www.reversemortgage.org.

AGE 65

THANKS TO LEGISLATION enacted in 2000, you can collect the full Social Security benefits you're eligible to receive regardless of whether you are working—or how much income you receive. The age of eligibility moves up to 67 by 2027 in two-month increments.

You're also now covered by Medicare. Don't worry, they will find you.

AGE 70½

ON APRIL 1 of the year after you turn 70½ you must start making required minimum withdrawals from your individual retirement accounts and also from your workplace retirement savings plans if you have stopped working. If you're still working, you can continue to contribute to—and postpone withdrawals from—your workplace plan as long as you do not own at least 5 percent of the company that employs you. If you decide to **ROLL OVER** your workplace savings into an IRA after age 70½, you must take your **REQUIRED MINIMUM DISTRIBUTION** before the rollover is completed or you will have made an ineligible contribution, subject to a 6 percent penalty. (Roth IRAs are different. You're not required to take a withdrawal ever in your lifetime from a Roth IRA.)

AGE 75

DID YOU SAVE MONEY in a 403(b) plan before 1986? You may have been able to postpone withdrawals on the money that was in your account as of December 31, 1986. Only that portion, and none of the subsequent earnings, qualify for this delay. For more detailed information, see Number 10.

When you begin to take minimum withdrawals from this portion of your savings at age 75, it will be subject to current required distribution rules like the rest of the account.

AGES 90 AND BEYOND

IF YOU HAVE BEEN setting aside money in a **TAX-DEFER-RED ANNUITY**—a smart thing to do if you have taken required distributions you don't need—you have hit the end of the line on **TAX-DEFERRED** growth. Depending on the state in which you live and your annuity provider's interpretation of the Internal Revenue Code, you must generally begin minimum withdrawals by age 90 from any annuities that you have purchased with **AFTER-TAX DOLLARS**.

And then Uncle Sam is off your back. If you file and pay your taxes every year, you can chuck your calendar and keep track of your own birthdays!

The Best Strategies for Handling Retirement Assets

14
Play It Smart with Your Social Security

You can receive Social Security income early or hold out for a higher benefit if you wait.

DESPITE THE WARNINGS about Social Security's impending insolvency, brighter prospects have been reported for the nation's universal insurance system in each of the past few years. In the late 1990s, it was widely reported that the so-called Social Security trust funds would run out in 2035. In 2000, that date was revised to 2038. Last year, it was raised to 2041. (It's my feeling that the trust funds will run out when the world's natural oil reserves are depleted. The two seem to follow the same path.)

The truth is that there are so many economic and demographic assumptions built into these estimates that a date will remain difficult to pin down. However, as financial pressure mounts when the baby boom generation begins to retire in about seven years, our predictive skills may improve.

An estimated 95 percent of all jobs in America are covered by Social Security. Whether you qualify to collect Social Security benefits depends on whether you have earned enough "credits." It really doesn't take much: You need forty credits, which amounts to ten years of minimal income, to qualify for retirement income benefits. The more you earn, the more you pay toward Social Security during your working years and the more you can expect to collect when you retire up to a point. However, in terms of income replacement, lower income workers can expect to replace a greater percentage of their income than higher income workers—an estimated 60 percent versus 25 percent for individuals who earn the maximum income subject to Social Security, which was $84,900 in 2002.

But here's your challenge in deciding what to do about Social Security: You can choose to retire as early as age 62 and begin to receive somewhat reduced benefits. You can work until your full retirement age, which is 65 for individuals born in 1935 or earlier, and collect higher benefits. (The age for collecting full benefits rises in two-month increments for individuals born in 1938 and after. It's age 67 if you were born after 1959—see the table on page 142.) Or, you can delay your benefits until you are 70 and receive a substantial increase over your full retirement benefit. Here's an example:

Sharon is 60 years old. She has just received a personalized statement from Social Security, which arrives each year several months before her birthday. It shows that with her job history—she's an executive with thirty years on the job at a computer company—and at her current salary, she will be entitled to the following three options (expressed in current dollars—the amounts rise with inflation), assuming that she continues to work and to earn at her current level until she begins to receive her benefits:

◆ **$1,248 per month** if she opts for early retirement at age 62

◆ **$1,560 per month** if she begins benefits at the full retirement age of 65

◆ **$2,047 per month** if she delays benefits until she is age 70. After 70, there's no further premium.

These projected benefits are the product of a complicated formula that takes into consideration Sharon's highest thirty-five years of income. Since Sharon has only worked full time at a relatively high-paying job for thirty years, her full retirement benefit could go up if she postponed retirement until age 65.

And, if she opts for early retirement benefits, she could lose most of her benefit if she continues to work. She would lose one dollar in benefits for every two dollars she earns above $11,500 at age 62. In the year before she turns 65, she would forfeit one dollar in every three earned above $30,000. After 65, she can continue to work and earn and receive $1,248 a month for life.

You don't need an advanced degree in statistics to see that choosing the early retirement benefit is not a very good deal unless you plan on keeping your earned income down. If you are healthy and active and you enjoy your work, it makes good sense to hang in there at least until full retirement age. And if you earn more than $30,000, you are better off pushing it off one more year until you are entitled to full benefits regardless of your income.

You can't get around these reductions in benefits by supplementing your Social Security income with withdrawals from your other savings or retirement plans. **CAPITAL GAINS**, dividends, interest income, and any withdrawals from your retirement plans or accounts count as income and you fail the test if you push past $11,500 or $30,000, regardless of its source.

NEXT QUESTION—65 OR 70?

DOES IT MAKE SENSE to delay your Social Security benefits? That larger sum payable from 70 on looks very tempting, but you should think twice before you choose the delayed benefit: It will take Sharon sixteen years of collecting the higher benefit to make up for the five years she forfeited by delaying her Social Security. Now that you can collect a full benefit after age 65, regardless of your income, it makes sense to take it and bank it if you don't really need it. Sharon could add another $95,000 or more to her retirement nest egg in her final five years of employment simply by investing her Social Security checks.

DON'T FORGET ABOUT TAXES

THE DECISION ABOUT when to take your Social Security benefits has one more wrinkle: taxes. If Social Security is only one component of your retirement income, as it is for more than half of all retired Americans, you are probably

SOCIAL SECURITY'S FULL RETIREMENT AGE IS RISING

IF YOU WERE BORN ...	YOU CAN RECEIVE BENEFITS WHEN YOU ARE AGE ...
after 1935	65
in 1938	65 + 2 months
1939	65 + 4 months
1940	65 + 6 months
1941	65 + 8 months
1942	65 + 10 months
1943–54	66
1955	66 + 2 months
1956	66 + 4 months
1957	66 + 6 months
1958	66 + 8 months
1959	66 + 10 months
after 1959	67

SOURCE: SOCIAL SECURITY ADMINISTRATION, 2002

going to lose some of your benefit to taxes. In fact, you don't have to be living the high life to find yourself paying income tax on nearly all of your benefit. If your household retirement income outside of Social Security tops $32,000, you'll pay income tax on 50 percent of your benefit. If your income exceeds $44,000, that percentage rises to 85 percent. Both amounts are adjusted from time to time for inflation.

Can you manage your Social Security strategy to minimize taxes? Probably not. If your income exceeds $44,000 and 85 percent of your Social Security benefit is subject to taxation, you can expect to lose something on the order of 25 percent of your benefits to taxes. It won't matter whether you take your benefits early, late, or on time.

NO DOUBLE-DIPPING

IF YOU HAVE WORKED for an employer that is not covered by Social Security—a state or federal government agency, for example, or a school district—but you have also paid into the Social Security system at another place of employment, you may think that you will be entitled to pension income from both. After all, you've contributed to both. However, Social Security doesn't see it this way. Even if you've had a summer job painting houses between your years of teaching, your credits virtually vanish because of a fancy formula that Social Security has worked out as part of what it calls its **WINDFALL ELIMINATION PROVISION**. No mention of the windfall the Social Security Administration received when it collected taxes from you and your employer over the years.

How to Choose—and When to Change— Your Investment Strategy

Your investment strategy in retirement should be realistic, optimistic, uncomplicated, and easy to execute.

WHAT SCARES YOU MOST about money and retirement? If you're like most Americans, I would guess that you worry about two things. First, making an investment decision that could wipe out your savings or cost you a level of comfort that you have been counting on. Less common is the fear of outliving your savings, i.e., running out of money because you live longer than you expected. Helping you avoid the first mistake is what this section is about. Helping you avoid the second is the subject of Number 16.

Choosing an investment strategy that can get you through retirement is both easier than you think and more difficult. Let me explain. It's easier because it depends on things most anyone can do on his or her own. It's harder because it means setting aside your fears—and most of what you hear in the press—and having the courage of your conviction once you put your strategy in place, even when the financial markets are going haywire as they have done since the Internet bubble burst in 2000.

A WINNING STRATEGY

MOST FINANCIAL EXPERTS agree that there are five things you should know to create a personal investment strategy in retirement. Because it is *personal,* I can't tell you exactly what your strategy should be. But I believe that if you incorporate these five points into your strategy, you will be on solid ground. Even if you plan to hire a professional to create a personal investment strategy for you, you should keep these five things in mind as you and your investment professional work together.

◆ **Invest in the stock market.** Any financial adviser will tell you that the only way to keep your retirement savings from running out in your lifetime is to choose a strategy that will keep you ahead of inflation. And that means investing in the stock market. How much depends primarily on your ability to stomach risk. If you can ignore the stock market's pattern of volatility, you could make a case for 100 percent stocks—and many financial advisers do. Stocks are the clear winner over the long term. According to Ibbotson Associates, a firm that tracks long-term investment performance, stocks averaged an annual return of 10.7 percent over the past seventy-six years. The next best performing asset class was long-term corporate bonds, which gained just over half as much, or 5.7 percent on average, each year. I think a 100 percent stock market strategy works best if you don't really need your retirement savings to cover your income needs: You can afford to ride out the down years.

A more reasonable approach for most investors is to go with the mix used by large pension funds, which is 60 percent stocks and 40 percent bonds. If you are the nervous type, even that may feel too rich. But if your portfolio has less than 60 percent exposure to the stock market, even in retirement, you risk falling behind in your later years. On the other hand, it's better to know your risk tolerance and to match your investment strategy to it. In the pecking order of things to avoid, settling for lower returns is one step up from risking a costly mistake that could result from adopting an approach that you are unlikely to stick with in a volatile market.

◆ **Aim for the middle.** Don't try to hit a home run. A successful retirement investment strategy isn't about stellar performance. It's about holding on to what you have and giving it a chance for modest, long-term growth so that you can generate the income you need or pass it on to your heirs. And it's about staying ahead of inflation, because what you need to live on twenty years from now will generally be twice what you will need today, assuming even just a modest level of inflation. Once you accept the fact that it is okay to have so-so investment performance, it also makes it a lot easier to choose investments. You don't need a double or a triple. You just have to be in the ballpark to win.

◆ **Pay attention to costs.** If you are going to target modest but reasonable returns on your investments, it's essential to buy cheap. That means choosing mutual funds with no-load or low **LOADS**; looking for reasonable **EXPENSE RATIOS**; favoring index funds, which are by definition low cost; and keeping all your transaction costs to a minimum by dealing with a discount or online broker. Unfortunately, investors who lack confidence often get nickel-and-dimed on all of these points. They pay too much up front. They pay too much each year. Then, when performance is disappointing, as it has been over the past three years, they bail out and sometimes pay again.

Especially if you pay for advice, it's important to understand what you are charged for, how much you are charged, and where the money goes. If you work with a fee-only financial adviser, you will either be charged a percent of your total assets or you will be assessed an annual service fee. Sometimes it's a combination of the two. Some fee-only planners will occasionally recommend a mutual fund that is sold with a sales charge if they think the fund's potential outweighs its entry fee. No reason to balk at this if you trust your adviser.

If you work with a broker, a financial company's sales representative, or an insurance agent selling investment products, keep in mind that these investment professionals have a financial incentive to sell products rather than to manage your investments. That doesn't mean you can't benefit from their help. But you should understand how they make their money. Your costs will generally be higher, but you will not know unless you ask.

◆ **Stick with your plan.** Be willing to invest some time in choosing an investment strategy. Then, once it is in place, stick with it. If you don't, you will almost surely saddle yourself with poor performance. Consider the results of a recent study of mutual fund trading patterns using data that spanned twenty years. The study was led by Gavin Quill, a senior vice president and director of research studies at Financial Research Corporation, who concluded that investors frequently behave in a way that undermines their long-term goals. "The overwhelming majority of investors say they adhere to a buy-and-hold philosophy," says Quill. Yet the evidence Quill and his research team assembled shows that investors lose a good portion of their potential returns because they trade excessively and their trades are poorly timed. What's more, the data show that trading activity has been on the rise. Despite the mutual fund industry's attempt to educate its customers, and despite ample evidence that more frequent trading results in lower returns, investors find it hard to accept the most basic precept of successful investing: buy and hold.

That said, every plan needs annual maintenance to keep proportions on target. If you decide to divide your portfolio 60/40 between stocks and bonds, you need to keep those proportions by **REBALANCING** when the market's action has shifted them by 5 percentage points or more. In a good year for stocks, for example, your portfolio could go from 60/40 to 67/33. At the end of the year, cut back your best-performing stock holdings and add to your bond holdings. When you rebalance in a tax-advantaged retirement account, there are no consequences. If you rebalance in a taxable account, you should take taxes into consideration when you make your move.

◆ **Don't fuss over security selection.** If you think that a successful investment strategy depends on your ability— or your financial adviser's ability—to discover the next Microsoft or to choose the hottest mutual fund, you have mistaken investing for gambling. If you have a solid investment strategy, security selection is not as important or as difficult as you think. You can engineer it into a research project if you enjoy it and you are knowledgeable enough to make a difference. Here's what I mean: If investing is something you really like to do, sit down at the Morningstar website and choose small, mid-, and large-cap funds with decent track records. Choose one that has a **GROWTH** style and one that has a **VALUE** approach. If you have an aggressive approach, include a technology fund and a health care fund to give your stock portfolio a bit of an edge. Keep in mind that your emphasis in this exercise should be on fine-tuning your asset class exposure, not on finding winning funds. Fund leadership changes rapidly. That said, there are a handful of funds that dominate their categories. Vanguard Health Care Fund comes to mind, and John Hancock Regional Bank Fund. After all your efforts, you should end up with a stock portfolio of between four and eight funds.

If investing is not something you want to spend much time on but you want a solid investment portfolio, take your 60 percent and invest it in Vanguard Total Market Index Fund and head for the pool. Or choose a core stock fund with a terrific long-term record, such as Fidelity Magellan Fund, Fidelity's flagship stock fund, or American Funds's Investment Company of America, which has experienced only one down year of performance in the past twenty-four years. Whether you have a carefully crafted multifund stock portfolio or a single, well-chosen fund, you have a reasonable investment strategy. And if you sit tight, you won't be a candidate for the next reality-based TV show, "Investors Behaving Badly," at some point along the way.

You can take a similar approach to your portfolio's bond position using mutual funds. If you choose a government securities fund, an investment grade bond fund, and a mortgage securities fund, you can cover three major domestic markets and get decent diversification. If you're comfortable with risk, you may want to add a high yield bond fund and/or an emerging markets bond fund. Both are risky, but if held in combination with the other types of bond funds, they offer diversification plus the potential for higher return over time. A simpler approach is to choose an income index fund or a strategic income fund that lets the fund manager divide assets among a variety of major markets. That way you don't have to worry about **REBAL-ANCING** among several funds.

Owning individual bonds, especially Treasuries, can also make sense. However, you are more likely to own these as part of your income portfolio than of your investment portfolio. It's hard to actively manage individual bonds as part of your investment portfolio. You're at a cost disadvantage to large institutions as soon as you move away from the Treasury market. Research is tough to do on your own, and transaction costs can be high.

CHANGING YOUR STRATEGY

IF YOU PUT an investment strategy in place at 65, should you change it as you get older? Age is only one factor in your strategy. A good rule of thumb is that you should change your strategy when the reasons you put it in place have themselves changed. So, what could those changes be?

◆ **You discover that your asset allocation is too aggressive for your risk tolerance** (or too conservative for your long-term income needs). Avoid making big changes in a single year. Shift gradually into a new allocation.

◆ **You no longer feel like managing your own portfolio.** You can simplify your **ASSET ALLOCATION**, or you can turn your portfolio over to an investment professional who may recommend a change in strategy.

◆ **You have reached an age where a severe stretch of negative stock market returns could hurt your ability to generate a predictable stream of income.** It may be time to cut back on your exposure to stocks and increase your investment in bonds.

◆ **As you approach your seventy-fifth birthday, you are concerned that your assets may not last your entire lifetime.** If you are just able to get by on the income you receive from your portfolio, it may be time to consider an annuity that can guarantee you income for life.

ADDITIONAL READING

MOST INVESTMENT COMPANIES offer model portfolios designed for investing in retirement. I don't find them very useful. They are typically labeled "conservative," "balanced," and "aggressive," or something close to that. But that begs the question of how well you know yourself and where you think you fit into those categories. If you want to read more about developing an investment strategy for retirement, take a look at *Investing During Retirement* by The Vanguard Group and published by Irwin Professional Publishing. It's available in paperback.

How to Create Your Income Strategy

Limit your first withdrawal to 3 percent to 5 percent and raise the dollar amount you withdraw to keep up with inflation.

CREATING AN INCOME STRATEGY is a two-step process. First, you need to determine how much income you can reasonably take from your retirement savings. Second, you need a plan to make the income available to you when you need it.

HOW MUCH CAN YOU WITHDRAW?

MOST FINANCIAL EXPERTS agree that the single biggest mistake people make with their retirement savings is to expect it to generate more income than is safe given the years they will likely spend in retirement. "People don't know the right amount of money to take out," says Deena Katz, a Florida-based certified financial planner and a partner at Evensky, Brown & Katz. "So they wind up taking out more than their portfolios can reasonably produce during the years they spend in retirement, and they run out of money."

So what's a reasonable withdrawal rate? Katz says something on the order of 3 percent to 5 percent. That number should be safe even if investment returns over the next decade are significantly lower than the 10.7 percent historical average. Also, it should allow you to raise the dollar amount you withdraw to keep pace with inflation.

The source of much wrong thinking about withdrawal rates, according to Katz, is the notion that you can "withdraw" at your portfolio's expected earnings rate. In other words, if you expect to earn 8 percent a year on your investments, you can afford to withdraw 8 percent a year. The flaw in that approach is twofold: Portfolios don't earn in a straight line, and if you begin retirement when the financial markets are in a funk—as they were from 2000 to 2002—you could wipe out your portfolio in no time. An 8 percent annual withdrawal from a $100,000 stock portfolio beginning in 2000 might have left you with about $53,358 by the end of 2002. Ready to go back to work?

YOUR INCOME PLAN

FINANCIAL EXPERTS NOW agree that you must separate your income strategy from your investment strategy, a departure from the conventional thinking of a generation ago. The old view was that you kept most of your retirement assets in bonds and you simply lived on the income they generated. Perhaps you included some dividend-generating stocks and dividend checks also became part of your income stream. But that's harder today because the dividend yield on the S&P 500 has declined from 5 percent in the 1970s to just over 1 percent in 2002.

With a portfolio that is more heavily invested in stocks, that doesn't work as well. You'll deprive yourself of income in the stock market's lean years and find yourself awash in cash in the fat years. Here's an approach recommended by Katz and many other top financial advisers: Create an income account and fund it with one year of cash (in a high-quality money market account) and two to three years of bonds, **LADDERED** to come due in each of the following years. Or divide the remaining amount between a short-term and an intermediate-term bond fund.

With three to four years of income in your account, you will shield your income plan from short-term market volatility. Any earnings on your income account can be plowed back into your income to provide an inflation raise for the following year. When you deplete a year of income, you'll add to your intermediate-term bonds or bond fund with dividends or income generated by your investment portfolio or by selling some of your assets during years when income and dividends are inadequate.

By keeping your investments separate from your income account, it will also be easier to stay on top of your strategic **ASSET ALLOCATION**. When **REBALANCING** to keep asset proportions on target, you can make your annual **TRANSFER** of income funds.

YOUR INCOME PLAN OVER TIME

TEN YEARS INTO RETIREMENT you may want to review your income and your investment strategies. If your investments are divided 60/40 between stocks and bonds, chances are that your wealth will have grown nicely if the markets perform in line with their historical averages. At that point, you may feel that you can consider giving yourself a raise. But be careful. It's better to have a little extra just in case the next decade is not as kind to your accounts. Or, you may want to start thinking in terms of your estate plan. If you can live on the income you're generating, why not think about leaving something behind?

If, however, your expenses have driven your income needs higher, and your primary concern is not running out of money, you may want to consider an annuity to cover your fixed expenses and to guarantee a source of lifetime income. A fixed annuity won't offer you exciting returns, but security may seem more attractive, especially if you find yourself on your own during your later years.

OTHER AVENUES TO INCOME

THE STRATEGY OUTLINED above assumes that you will take charge of creating your own retirement paycheck. There are other ways to go. You can roll your retirement savings over into an **INCOME ANNUITY** to cover your expenses without the worry of outliving your income. Or, you could opt for a **SYSTEMATIC WITHDRAWAL PROGRAM**, which may be offered by your mutual fund company or your 401(k). A systematic withdrawal program is nothing more than an actuarially sound draw-down of your savings—you can think of it as self-made annuity allowing you the flexibility to change your mind at any time. Katz is lukewarm on systematic withdrawal programs because they could shorten the expected life of your portfolio if you start withdrawals in a high-return environment and then the markets suddenly shift lower.

17

When an Annuity Makes Sense

An annuity can guarantee you income for life, but costs and the health of the issuer vary widely.

THE STOCK MARKET VOLATILITY of the early twenty-first century has earned annuities new respect. All of a sudden the notion of guaranteed lifetime income based on a relatively modest return doesn't sound so bad.

Do you need an annuity in your retirement income plan? If you work with a fee-only financial planner, it is unlikely to show up on a list of recommendations. There's nothing in it for a planner who makes his or her money from assets under management to suggest that you remove a big chunk of that money and use it to buy an annuity. Besides, most planners feel they can create an income plan with all the features of an annuity. That's what you're paying for.

But if you're the independent sort, and you are taking charge of your own retirement paycheck, an annuity is worth considering for at least a portion of your income plan. It can guarantee income for life. It can offer income that can grow over time, if you're willing to assume some risk. But you should do your homework before you purchase an annuity. Here's what you should know before you begin your search.

INCOME ANNUITY BASICS

AN **INCOME ANNUITY** IS *not* an investment. And it's different from a **TAX-DEFERRED ANNUITY**, which is designed primarily to accumulate additional tax-deferred savings for individuals who have maxed out on other tax-advantaged retirement savings plans. An income annuity is a contract between you and an insurance company. You "purchase" an annuity with an amount of money—$10,000 is a typical minimum; $100,000 is a more typical purchase. In return, the insurance company agrees to pay you regular income over a specified period of time, based on your age and gender and the purchase amount. You can purchase an annuity that will pay income over your entire lifetime, your lifetime in combination with another person's, or a specific term—ten or twenty years, for example.

If you have money saved in a 401(k), a 403(b), a 457 plan, or any other type of tax-advantaged retirement savings plan, you can roll it over to an income annuity. You can **ROLL OVER** a **LUMP SUM DISTRIBUTION** from a pension plan. Or, you can take any sum of money and purchase an income annuity outright. But your source of funds matters: Money that comes from another tax-advantaged plan will be taxed as **ORDINARY INCOME** as you withdraw it and your income stream will be designed to take into account required minimum withdrawals after age 70½. Money that comes either from a deferred annuity that you have decided to convert to an income annuity or from other after-tax savings will be subject to tax only on earnings, and you can postpone required minimum withdrawals until you are 90.

Income annuities come in two basic varieties. When you purchase a **FIXED INCOME ANNUITY**, the interest rate is set for the life of the annuity. It figures into the calculation of your income payment, along with your age and gender, the purchase amount, and the term you choose. With interest rates as low as they have been for decades, the income paid from a $100,000 fixed income lifetime annuity purchased from Fidelity Investments Life Insurance Company by a 65-year-old single male has dropped from $923 a month in 1991 to $755 a month in 2002, something to keep in mind before you lock yourself into a fixed income annuity payment for life. On the other hand, if your other sources of income are inadequate to cover your estimated routine expenses, a fixed annuity will guarantee that you will never fall short—and you will never outlive your income if you choose an annuity that covers your lifetime.

If you can accept some fluctuation in your monthly income, you may find the long-term income growth potential of a **VARIABLE INCOME ANNUITY** more attractive than the fixed variety. A variable annuity offers the opportunity for a rising income stream if the "investment portfolios" you choose do well. A good variable income annuity will offer a wide choice of investment options to pick from, similar to a menu of mutual funds. It's a good idea to allocate money among a variety of asset types (stocks, bonds, etc.) so that you won't take on too much risk for your retirement years.

Understanding how the income on your variable annuity is calculated is just a little tricky. In addition to the factors that figure into a fixed income annuity income payment calculation—age, gender, etc.—you will be asked to choose a **BENCHMARK RATE OF RETURN**, which is also called the assumed interest rate for your annuity. This figure does two things: It establishes the amount of your first payment, and it establishes a standard or hurdle rate for future payments. After your first payment, your income will increase, decrease, or stay the same depending on whether the investments you have chosen for your annuity beat the benchmark. Most companies offer two or three rates, which might range from 2.5 percent to 7 percent. In some states, high benchmarks are not permitted.

If you pick a lower rate, the amount of income you receive may be slightly lower at the outset, but both potential gains and the rate at which your income can rise are greater going forward. At the higher rate, your initial income amount is larger, but your portfolio will have to perform significantly better to reap larger gains going forward.

The way the benchmark is applied to the actual dollar amount of income you receive is not entirely transparent. Any change in the performance of the investment portfolios you select will change the income you receive by the same percentage, minus the benchmark rate and annuity expenses. However, the actual dollars are spread out over the life of the contract to help provide some downside protection.

An income annuity statement is not all that easy to understand. Your purchase buys you **ANNUITY UNITS**, similar to mutual fund shares, which remain a constant number over the period of time you collect income. The value of the units changes based on the performance of the portfolios you choose and your benchmark. To determine your income payments, you multiply the annuity value for each investment portfolio by the number of annuity units you own.

BUYER BEWARE

A FEW THINGS you should know about income annuities:

◆ **Buy a fixed income annuity from an insurance company with an A+ rating** from A.M. Best's Rating Service, which you can find on the Web at www.ambest.com. The solvency of your insurance company really matters. If the insurance company falls on hard times, the reserves it uses to pay its contract holders could be subject to the demands of creditors. Variable income annuities offer some protection in this regard because your money is put into a separate account and you control how your annuity is invested.

◆ **The purchase of an income annuity is an irrevocable decision.** You can't get your money back. You can't **TRANSFER** it if you're dissatisfied with returns. With a variable income annuity, you do have the opportunity to reallocate your assets, which can have an impact on your income. But because your benchmark rate is locked in, reallocation during rocky times in the market may not help raise your income.

Some variable income annuities have recently been adding features to make annuities more palatable. A "liquidity" feature, for example, allows the annuity owner to get access to cash for additional withdrawals. However, this flexibility isn't free. Annuities with liquidity options cost more or reduce the income payout.

◆ **Cost really matters.** If you work with a financial planner who collects fees based on the products he or she sells, or one who is associated with an insurance company, you can expect that a healthy percentage of your annuity's purchase price will go toward compensating the seller. Stick with low-fee annuities from companies such as Fidelity, Vanguard, T. Rowe Price, and TIAA-CREF.

◆ **Fancy annuity features come at a price.** Most low-cost companies also keep the bells and whistles to a minimum. The more options you add to an annuity, the lower your payout or the higher your fee. Period.

◆ **Don't put too much of your savings into an annuity.** Think of an annuity as your own private pension plan. Think of it as a way of covering your fixed expenses. But don't lock up all of your retirement savings in an annuity. Farrell Dolan, executive vice president at Fidelity Investments Life Insurance Company, says the typical customer puts about 25 percent of his or her retirement assets into annuities— a reasonable guideline.

When a Roth IRA Conversion Makes Sense

It's a great, tax-savvy way to pass on wealth to your heirs. But the window of opportunity for conversion may be small.

WHEN ROTH IRAS were introduced in the late 1990s, they offered retirement savers an interesting option: The money contributed to a Roth IRA isn't **TAX DEDUCTIBLE**, as it may be with a traditional IRA. But after five years, withdrawals are tax free for anyone age 59½ or older. So what we're talking about here is tax-free growth and tax-free income for life.

There's one more advantage to a Roth IRA. There are no required minimum withdrawals. So you could conceivably let your money grow in a Roth tax free for as long as you live, then pass on whatever is left to your heirs. They will be required to withdraw a minimum amount each year, based on their own life expectancies, but both earnings growth and withdrawals are still tax free. And that turns out to be a very big deal over time.

ROTH'S VALUE AS WORK ENDS

BUT WHY TALK about the advantages of a Roth IRA when your saving days come to an end? It's not the accumulation features that are appealing once you retire, but rather the potential a Roth IRA offers for retirement savings that you may have earmarked for your estate plan. If you envision leaving an inheritance for your children or grandchildren—and if you have the financial resources to pay your tax bill up front—a **CONVERSION** to a Roth IRA could make sense. Here's why: If you have a choice of assets to pass on to your heirs, a Roth IRA can solve two tax problems in one move. By paying the tax on assets converted to a Roth IRA, you will remove money from your estate that might have been subject to federal estate tax. (The estate tax is scheduled to disappear in 2010, but don't count on it.) Plus, you'll pass on an asset that is worth its full value. If you pass on any other type of IRA or a 401(k), it will be subject to income tax.

Consider this example: Because you have adequate retirement income between your pension and Social Security, you don't need to touch the million dollars you've accumulated in your IRA or the $350,000 you've set aside in personal savings. If you die with these accounts in place, your heirs will owe estate tax of approximately $140,000 on the amount of your estate in excess of $1 million—in this case, $350,000. Plus, there would be a federal income tax bill due of $246,000—at the highest current rate of 38.6 percent minus a credit for the estate tax paid. So what do your heirs actually get?

Your Current Estate

$	350,000	personal savings
$	1,000,000	IRA
$ 1,350,000		**Total assets**
–	140,000	federal estate tax
–	246,000	federal income tax minus credit for estate tax paid
$	**964,000**	**Total to your heirs**

Look what happens if you convert your $1 million to a Roth IRA during your lifetime. You'll owe federal income tax of $385,000 in the year that you convert. That will wipe out your $350,000 savings and require that you kick in something from your budget during the year you convert.

If you passed away that same year, your transaction may appear to be a wash.

Your Estate with a Roth IRA Conversion

$	350,000	personal savings
$	1,000,000	IRA
$ 1,350,000		**Total assets**
–	385,000	federal income tax on conversion to Roth IRA
–	0	federal estate tax
$	**965,000**	**Total to your heirs**

Because the only asset in your estate is now your Roth IRA, you'll owe *no* federal estate tax. (You can pass on $1 million estate tax free in 2003, an amount that rises to $1.5 million in 2004 and $3.5 million in 2009.) But you're only $1,000 ahead with a Roth IRA conversion. And you've depleted your personal savings.

Here's the other side: You can always tap your Roth IRA if you need it in an emergency. And for every year that you live, the value of your Roth IRA has the potential to grow tax free. If your Roth IRA is worth $1.5 million in five years, your entire estate passes both estate and federal income tax free to your heirs. Without the conversion, your estate tax bill would have disappeared, but the federal income tax due on your appreciated IRA would have risen to $525,000 and you would pass on $175,000 less to your heirs.

TWO STEPS TO A ROTH IRA

YOU CAN CONVERT any type of traditional IRA—a contributory IRA, a SEP IRA, or a rollover IRA—directly to a Roth IRA by filing the paperwork with your investment company. Today, most companies will let you complete the process online. Going from your retirement plan savings to a Roth IRA is a two-step process. First you have to **ROLL OVER** to an IRA, and then you can convert some or all of your assets to a Roth IRA.

There are some strings attached. Your income can't exceed $100,000 in the year you convert, whether you are single or married. That shouldn't be a real obstacle, because with a little ingenuity, even individuals with significant annual income can manage it down to $100,000 in their last calendar year of employment.

But there is one way to get stuck, and it has to do with the timing of your conversion: If you wait until you turn 70½, you may be ineligible to convert if the amount that you are required to take as a minimum distribution from your IRA would push you over the $100,000 eligibility mark. Your **REQUIRED MINIMUM DISTRIBUTION** counts against the $100,000 Roth IRA conversion eligibility limit and the IRS says you can't roll it over. In fact, you may be out of luck even if you aren't actually required to take your first minimum distribution until next year (because you turned 70½ this year). The IRS takes the position that your first distribution is actually *due* in the year you turn 70½ even if it isn't *payable* until the following year.

This wrinkle is scheduled to disappear in 2005, after which your required minimum distribution would be excluded from the $100,000 Roth eligibility test. But for the next few years, it makes sense to play it safe. If a Roth IRA conversion makes sense, do it now.

NO WEALTH, NO WAY

WHAT IF YOU'RE JUST John Q. Average with a modest amount in your IRA? Does a Roth IRA conversion ever make sense? Most financial experts say "forget it." You would have to use your taxable savings to pay the conversion tax bill. That runs counter to sound advice to tap your taxable savings first for your own needs whenever you can. Second, since your tax bill should go lower in retirement, you'll often find yourself paying more in income tax than you might had you postponed the tax bill. And that's really the point. With a Roth IRA, you are forced to pay taxes sooner than later. Unless you have a reason, why do it?

When You Don't Need Your Retirement Savings for Income

You need a special strategy to maximize wealth transfer and minimize taxes.

LUCKY YOU. You set aside money for retirement, nurtured it to make it grow, and now you find that your other income resources will cover your needs. Now you'll preserve as much as you can for your heirs. But here's the problem. Your retirement savings are like the Trojan horse. Inside is an enormous tax bill waiting for the person who opens the door. You have some options in terms of how taxes are paid and when. The time to tackle them is early in your retirement so that you will have maximum flexibility in executing a strategy.

Financial planners offer many strategies for retirement savings plans with big balances and no income demands, but these three lead the list.

◆ **Delay your withdrawals as long as possible** so that your account continues to build maximum value through **TAX-DEFERRED** growth. When you turn 70½, generally speaking you'll be required to begin minimum withdrawals.

◆ **Consider using your minimum withdrawals to purchase life insurance for an irrevocable life insurance trust,** if you have an estate that is valued at more than $1 million. The insurance will be available to offset the estate tax that will be due upon your death and the income tax that will be due when your heirs begin withdrawals from the retirement savings they inherit from you.

If your estate is worth less than $1 million, federal estate tax is unlikely to be an issue. Consider using your required withdrawals to establish Roth IRAs for your working grand-children. You can put away up to $3,000 a year for anyone who has earned income within the eligibility require-ments. Someday, your grandchild will have the luxury of tax-free withdrawals thanks to you!

◆ **Convert your retirement savings to a Roth IRA** if you can manage your income down to no more than $100,000 in your last year of employment—and before you turn 70. You'll pay the tax bill up front and pass a tax-free asset on to your heirs. (For more information, see Number 18.)

If you don't need your retirement savings for income, you should also try to maintain an aggressive investment strategy. Even if you're conservative by nature, you're in an ideal position to take risk with your retirement savings. You don't need them to live on. You can afford to turn them over to the market and ride out any downturn. This is an opportunity often missed by individuals of modest means who have a few bucks stashed in an IRA. Even if you look at it as a source of funds for an emergency, you can afford to take risks with this money. It's not outrageous to put 100 percent of it in the stock market.

Special
Situations

Early Withdrawals from Your Retirement Savings

You can get around the 10 percent penalty tax.

IF YOU ARE THINKING about retiring before the traditional age of 65—or if you find yourself out of work before you expected—you may need to tap your tax-advantaged retirement savings for income. But there is the small matter of a 10 percent early withdrawal penalty that generally applies to money withdrawn from tax-advantaged retirement savings plans before age 59½ (or age 55, if your employer lets you go). You can get around the penalty, regardless of your age, by following IRS guidelines to create a steady stream of income called **SUBSTANTIALLY EQUAL PAYMENTS** [or Section 72(t) withdrawals] from one or more of your retirement savings accounts.

But here's the catch: This is not a casual arrangement. There are three approved formulas for calculating the amount of your withdrawals, which the IRS refers to as payments. Once you start, you can't stop or change the payments for five years or until you are 59½, whichever is longer, unless you die or you are disabled. And you can't use this option to withdraw money from a workplace retirement savings plan while you are still employed, although you can get at your IRA savings regardless of your employment status. If you fail to follow these rules, the 10 percent penalty applies to all your withdrawals retroactively along with interest as far back as an infraction occurred.

THREE WAYS TO CALCULATE
YOUR PAYMENTS

THE IRS GUIDELINES for computing the amount of money you can withdraw are fairly detailed, but they leave some items open to interpretation, as you will see in the discussions below. Even where there appears to be some latitude, it's a good idea to err on the side of caution. The aim of the guidelines is to give you access to your savings but only in a manner that would spread them evenly over your lifetime. And the conventional wisdom is that you should avoid manipulating the guidelines to generate an overly large payment amount.

◆ **Minimum distribution method.** You can calculate your payments using the rules that govern **REQUIRED MINIMUM DISTRIBUTIONS**. That means using your life expectancy, as determined by the IRS-approved single- or joint-life expectancy tables (see pages 186 and 106–107, respectively) and the value of your account as of December 31 of the previous year to determine your payment. (Most individuals choose the single-life expectancy table because it produces a larger payment.) You simply divide your account balance by your life expectancy as if you were calculating a required minimum distribution.

Your account balance on December 31	$100,000
Your life expectancy at age 50	34.2 years
Your first annual payment	**$2,923.98**

Because your account balance will change from year to year, the amount you pay yourself using this method will vary, too. Just keep in mind that you must take the precise amount that results from this calculation—no more, no less.

◆ **Amortization method.** This one offers flexibility that you don't get with the **MINIMUM DISTRIBUTION METHOD** plus the opportunity to generate a higher annual payment.

It allows you to choose an interest rate that figures into your calculation. The IRS doesn't specify the rate, only that it should be reasonable. Because higher rates result in higher payments, it's a good idea to avoid anything that is really high. Most financial practitioners who use this calculation say that they are comfortable with something that approximates the interest rate on long-term U.S. Treasuries or 120 percent of the rate on intermediate-term Treasuries.

This way doesn't require that you value your account on December 31 of the prior year, which has left some gray area for using an alternate date, such as the month before your first payment, if it would help you generate a higher payment and if that is your goal.

You calculate your annual withdrawal as if it were a mortgage payment to yourself and as if your life expectancy from the IRS-approved tables were the term of the loan. For example:

Your account balance on December 31	$100,000
Your interest rate 6.0 percent	
Your life expectancy at age 50	34.2 years
Your annual payment	**$6,891.00**

The calculation feels more cumbersome than it actually is in a world of online calculators. The one at www.nolo.com in the site's small business center is a good one to use because it will let you put in a long series of payments. Traditional mortgage calculators won't go beyond thirty years, which may not be long enough if you are doing this calculation at age 55.

You aren't likely to find a calculator that will handle a fraction of a month. And because it is important to be precise about your calculation, it's a good idea to use an online calculator for a ballpark estimate of your payment. Have an accountant run your final number so that you don't fudge it even a penny.

When you use the amortization payment, the amount of your annual income doesn't change from year to year. On one hand, that's good. You don't have to repeat the calculation. However, you may feel somewhat boxed in if your account value moves up smartly, inflation puts a squeeze on your budget, and your annual payment is fixed for five years or more.

◆ **Annuity method.** A third option introduces one more element of flexibility. As with the amortization method, you choose an interest rate to use in your calculation, but the annuity method gives you a choice of life expectancy tables to use. You can use the life expectancy assumptions used by insurance companies or large pension plans instead of the IRS table. These life expectancies, plus the interest rate you choose, are then translated into an "annuity factor," which you will use to calculate your payment. You divide your account balance by the annuity factor that matches up to your life expectancy and choice of interest rates from the annuity factor table.

Your account balance on December 31	$100,000
Your annuity factor (age 50, 6.0 percent)	12.7497
Your first annual payment	**$7,843.32**

Officially, the only difference between the amortization and the annuity factor is the table that you use, which may be significant in and of itself because it offers the opportunity for the highest payment of all three methods. In fact, it may offer a substantially higher payment for men because insurance company annuity factor tables are gender-specific, which the standard IRS tables are not. And because men have shorter life expectancies, they can generally calculate the highest possible payment using an insurance company annuity factor table.

There's one more consideration, albeit an unofficial one: Recent private letter rulings suggest that the IRS has been willing to let individuals use the annuity factor table to generate a payment that changes each year by employing the key features of the minimum distribution method —recalculation of life expectancies and the use of updated account balances. Although there is no guarantee that the IRS will take this stand on each case it considers, it is good to know how it has leaned on other cases. The opportunity to change your payments each year can be important in a good market, because it would allow you to take out an increasing amount of money from your account. But it would be especially valuable in a bad market, where you might otherwise be locked into a high annual payment from an account that has been decimated by a sinking stock market. For example, if you started a series of **SUBSTANTIALLY EQUAL PAYMENTS** from an IRA worth $500,000 in 2001, using the annuity factor method, you might have figured that you could withdraw about $38,000 a year. But now that your IRA is worth only $300,000, it may be worth it to look for a way to reduce that payment.

You can also satisfy the annuity method by purchasing an annuity with your retirement savings. The insurance company has some flexibility in structuring your payments, which may result in a slightly higher payout than you could achieve on your own in the early years. The drawback is that you lose the flexibility to cease income at some point if you find you don't really need it.

MORE—OR LESS

YOU WILL ACHIEVE a higher annual payment from your account by using your life expectancy alone and a lower payment by using your life expectancy with that of a younger **BENEFICIARY**. But the calculation has to reflect the age of your actual beneficiary.

You'll end up with a smaller payment if you isolate one account for substantially equal payments and leave your others alone. But if it meets your needs, it's a good way to get around certain rules. For example, if you are still working, you can't tap your 401(k). But you could take annual payments from your IRA. If you have a large IRA, you could split it into two accounts, size one for the annual payments you'd like to receive, and leave the other one alone.

Company Stock in Your Retirement Accounts

You could reduce your tax bill by more than one-third on company stock in your retirement account, but consider the risks before you choose this option.

IF YOU OWN SHARES of your employer's stock in a **QUALIFIED RETIREMENT PLAN** such as a 401(k), pension, **PROFIT SHARING**, or **EMPLOYEE STOCK OWNERSHIP PLAN (ESOP)**, you may be entitled to a special tax break when it is time to withdraw your savings. This special break is available to anyone who is leaving a job or retiring at age 59½ or over. It's also available to anyone who is disabled or to heirs who inherit retirement savings that are invested in an employer's stock.

But you have to follow some fairly strict rules to qualify. You must take 100 percent of the balance of the tax-advantaged plan that holds your employer stock and all in the same taxable year—unless you bought the stock with **AFTER-TAX DOLLARS**, in which case you can qualify for special tax treatment even if you take only a portion of your stock. But if the stock is in a plan on which taxes have not been withheld, you have to take all the money out of your plan and from any other similar retirement plans (for example, a pension plan, a profit sharing plan, or a stock bonus plan).

You have some options as to how to treat the other investments in these plans. For example, if you own mutual funds in your 401(k) and employer stock in your profit sharing plan, you can **ROLL OVER** the fund shares to an IRA. You can even roll over some of your employer stock.

But in order to qualify for special tax treatment you must take the remaining portion of your employer stock **IN KIND**. That is, you simply move your shares from your retirement account to an account at a financial company of your choice. You can't sell your shares and take the cash, and you can't roll them over into an IRA.

What do you get if you follow these strict rules? A lower tax rate on a portion of the appreciation on your employer stock called **NET UNREALIZED APPRECIATION**, or **NUA**. The financial industry loves acronyms, even if they aren't all that friendly to the customer.

Let me try to explain why NUA can be a big deal: Generally speaking, when you withdraw money from your tax-advantaged retirement savings accounts, it is taxed as **ORDINARY INCOME**. Most of it has been shielded from taxes on its way into your accounts. It was invested before it passed through your paycheck. Now it's time to pay the piper. Regardless of how your accounts have grown—through interest income, dividends, or **CAPITAL GAINS**—it's all taxed as ordinary income when it comes out. That is, unless it qualifies for an exception such as NUA. Then, some portion of your assets—specifically your employer stock—can be taxed at the long-term capital gains rate of 20 percent, far lower than most ordinary income tax rates.

This exception, it turns out, could translate into a considerable tax savings. But it takes a leap of faith and a healthy reserve fund to take advantage of it. It's also one of those things that often looks better on paper than when you're actually faced with the decision about your own account. What's more, it really only works for individuals who have company stock that has appreciated significantly—like tenfold, not an outrageous proposition if you have worked for Microsoft or even for an old-line company such as Procter & Gamble.

Have I lost you? Look at this example. You have worked for Gillette for thirty years, and during that time you have participated in the company's ESOP, purchasing the company's stock each month. Now, at age 65, you are ready to retire, and you want to make the most of the 10,000 shares of Gillette stock you have accumulated. The stock is worth $650,000. But your **COST BASIS**, as reported to you by Gillette, is a mere $120,000. If you withdraw your shares and deposit them into an investment account at a **FINAN-CIAL SUPERMARKET** or brokerage, you will owe income tax on your $120,000 cost basis. If you're married and you file a joint tax return, that's enough to push you into the 30 percent marginal tax bracket even if your annual paycheck is $60,000. Of the $40,390 you'll pay to Uncle Sam that year, $34,000 will be income tax on the stock you withdraw. (This is where the reserve fund comes in. You'll have to put your hands on the money to pay the extra taxes.) But then, you won't owe another dime in taxes until you sell your stock. And if and when you do, anything above your cost basis, i.e., $12 a share, will be taxed at the long-term capital gains rate of 20 percent.

Why is this a good deal? Because you'll avoid paying all of your taxes at ordinary income tax rates, which can go as high as 38.6 percent in 2003.

◆ **If you withdraw your 10,000 shares and sell them,** you'll owe ordinary income tax on the full market value of $650,000. In 2003, that would leave you with a tax bill of $235,000 because more than half of your account is taxed at the highest marginal tax rate of 38.6 percent.

◆ **If you take the shares in kind,** you'll pay ordinary income tax at a marginal rate of 30 percent on your cost basis, as above, of $34,000. Plus, you'll owe long-term capital gains tax on the net unrealized appreciation when you sell your shares. At $65 a share, your capital gains tax bill would be $106,000 for a total tax bill of $140,000, or what appears to be a total tax savings of $95,000.

Wouldn't it make sense to choose the option that would save you $95,000? Well, not so fast. Marcia Mantell, a vice president at Fidelity Investments (in charge of the marketing program that explains these accounts to investors), says that it can be a very hard sell. Mantell says Fidelity gets a lot of phone calls, especially from technology company employees who have done well over the past fifteen to twenty years. "Even with the market downturn, a lot of people have multimillion-dollar accounts," says Mantell. But they balk at the fact that they have to put out some tax money now for a tax savings in the future. If they take advantage of this thing called NUA, they give up tax deferral and the option of delaying taxes until they begin withdrawals.

In addition, there are some real risks to be considered when you go the route of an in kind **DISTRIBUTION** to hold on to your company stock in retirement. When you remove your assets from the secure surrounding of a 401(k) or even an IRA, your assets are exposed to litigation and to the claims of creditors, against which they are generally protected when they are part of a qualified plan. Even IRAs have claims protection in many states. Then, there's the risk associated with owning a big position in a single security and the future investment risk of owning it for a very long time. You want to feel very good about your company's prospects over the long term.

Finally, there's the matter of your future tax bracket. Although today's highest bracket is 38.6 percent, you could conceivably stay in the 15 percent tax bracket if you roll your $650,000 into an IRA where it will continue to grow **TAX DEFERRED**, keep your withdrawals to $30,000 a year, and collect modest Social Security. Now the fancy tax footwork offered by NUA doesn't look as good, says Randall Smith, a CPA with Samet & Company, in Chestnut Hill, Massachusetts, who was kind enough to run these numbers.

OTHER CONSIDERATIONS

AN EARLY DISTRIBUTION of company stock is subject to the same 10 percent early withdrawal penalty tax that applies to any other early withdrawal. Likewise, some additional special tax treatments, such as the ability to use **TEN-YEAR FORWARD AVERAGING** to achieve a lower tax payment on the cost basis of your shares, is available to individuals who were born before January 1, 1936. You may also be eligible to use the 20 percent long-term capital gains tax on assets you accumulated before 1974 if you were born before January 1, 1936.

This is a lot to digest in a few thousand words. Consider this: If you own a large position in your employer's stock and it is worth at least twice as much as you paid for it, schedule a session with a tax adviser who professes to know the ins and outs of retirement income planning before you make any decision about your stock. Lay out your situation and ask for an analysis of your options. Some investment companies have developed special programs to handle your kind of situation, but the talent is very spotty. And the penalty for making a mistake with your account is unattractive. If you cash in even a few hundred shares to celebrate your retirement, you could lose your eligibility for these special tax treatments.

For Women Only

Women fall behind during their retirement savings years and need strategies to catch up because they live longer than men.

DIFFERENCES BETWEEN men and women are magnified in retirement. One older woman out of four lives at or near the poverty level, according to the Older Women's League—double the number of men. Less than half of all working women participate in a pension plan. And because women tend to work fewer years and more of them in part-time jobs, they are also less likely to qualify for a pension, even if they work for an employer who offers one. Only 30 percent of all women aged 65 or older actually collect a pension, compared to 48 percent of all men, and the pensions they collect are worth less than half of those paid to men. What's more, studies of women's investment patterns suggest that they invest more conservatively than men and end up with smaller nest eggs for retirement. Yet, the Department of Labor points out that a female retiring at age 65 can expect to live for approximately twenty more years—four years longer than a male retiring at the same age.

If your retirement profile is consistent with these factors, it is too late to turn back the clock. But there are some things that you can—and should—do as you prepare for retirement:

◆ **If you are married, pay attention to your spouse's retirement options.** If he is entitled to a pension, he is required to choose a joint-and-survivor option that would continue payment to you if you survive him. Don't waive that right unless you have a pension source of your own.

◆ **If you separate or divorce, insist on a QUALIFIED DOMES-TIC RELATIONS ORDER (QDRO)** to establish your right to a portion of your spouse's **QUALIFIED PLAN** retirement assets. It will ensure that any split of assets will take place without the loss of tax advantages. Without a QDRO, any transfer of assets from your spouse to your name from your spouse's name to yours could be subject to income tax and a 10 percent early withdrawal penalty, unless you are age 59½ or older. And because a QDRO must be written to meet criteria established by Congress, it enjoys special federal protection: It takes precedence over any other claims on your spouse's assets, including a tax lien from the IRS. (A QDRO won't apply to any savings your spouse has in an IRA. Those have to be handled separately.)

◆ **Review your asset allocation.** If you have been too conservative during your saving years, consider a more aggressive strategy for retirement. With a longer life expectancy, you need stocks in your portfolio.

◆ **Consider an annuity to cover your basic income needs.** Especially if you are a single woman, you don't need to worry about providing for a spouse or leaving something behind. An annuity is an insurance policy in reverse. It can insure against outliving your savings.

When Your Partner Is Not Your Spouse

A domestic partnership agreement affords protection when you are separated by death.

IF YOU SHARE your life with a partner to whom you are not married, you may have already grappled with financial situations in which you do not have the same protections given to married couples. If you have been casual about your assets, this is a good time to take a more organized approach.

Start by identifying a financial planner who can review a list of items that are pertinent to your retirement income and assets as they fit into your estate. Find someone who is sensitive to your situation as well as knowledgeable about your needs. How can you tell? John LeBlanc, principal at Back Bay Financial Group in Boston, has taken care that the group's brochures and marketing materials avoid the use of the terms *husband, wife,* and *spouse.* In their place, he uses *client* and *partner* to signal that they are comfortable working with nontraditional couples.

LeBlanc recommends that partners write a **DOMESTIC PARTNERSHIP AGREEMENT** to spell out the extent of their financial relationship. A properly worded agreement can help avoid any problems or disappointments that can arise when two people own investments, real estate, artwork, and vehicles together. In the agreement, you can list items that you consider joint property. Don't assume that everything will simply work itself out. Your partner's family will almost certainly get any assets that are not properly identified.

A partnership agreement can also include **BENEFICIARY** arrangements for retirement plan assets or life insurance policies, but the beneficiary form takes precedence over all other documentation for qualified retirement plan assets. Make sure you keep it up to date and that you have identified **CONTINGENT BENEFICIARIES**. That way, if something happens to you and your partner, you are still the one who will determine the ultimate destination of your retirement savings. If you name only your partner as your beneficiary, your partner's next of kin will become your beneficiary—which may not be what you had in mind.

If your partner is entitled to a pension from a long-time employer, he or she can name you as the person to receive income if your partner passes away before you. Especially if there is a disparity between income-earning power and personal assets, a joint-and-survivor annuity from a pension plan can help fill the gap.

And because unmarried couples do not qualify for the the **UNLIMITED MARITAL DEDUCTION**, which allows one member of a married couple to pass on an unlimited amount of money and assets to the other free of estate tax (as long as the spouse is an American citizen), it's especially important to get financial advice if either or both of you have accumulated significant assets in a retirement plan. If you have other assets to draw on in retirement, one strategy is to use withdrawals from your retirement assets after age 59½ to make the maximum allowable annual gift to your partner—$11,000 a year.

If you have children as well as partnership considerations, your affairs are further complicated. For example, if you and your partner own a home together but you each want your respective children to inherit it someday, you can create a **LIFE ESTATE**, which would allow the surviving partner the use of the house for the rest of his or her lifetime, then pass it on to both of your children. Or, you can purchase life insurance to cover the mortgage. The last thing you want is to leave your partner in a situation where he or she can't afford to buy out your portion of the house and is at the mercy of your children.

24

When You Inherit Retirement Assets

Two imperatives: preserve the tax-deferred growth, and don't touch a penny until you know the rules.

BECAUSE IRAs AND 401(K)s have now been around for twenty to twenty-five years, the generation that is just about to retire is the first to experience the challenge of a retirement inheritance. In fact, the odds are pretty good that there is a retirement inheritance in your future. What will you do with it?

I don't mean, will you spend it on a new car? Or add it to your son's college savings account? I mean, what will you *do*? Here's a fairly typical situation. You're 55. Sadly, your father passes away, your last living parent. You and your 45-year-old sister are the **DESIGNATED BENEFICIA- RIES** of your father's IRA. When you call the brokerage company that is the custodian of your father's account, you learn that it was worth $70,000 as of his last monthly statement.

Now what? Before you pay a visit to your father's broker, here are some general guidelines that you should keep in mind. [For practical purposes, these guidelines apply primarily to traditional IRAs, sort of by default. They could apply to money you inherit from a 401(k), but most workplace retirement savings plans will give beneficiaries one shot at taking the money out of the plan. As a result, many of the strategies discussed below are really only applicable to IRAs, although the comments about taxes apply to most all tax-advantaged plans and accounts.]

TAXES

IN ADDITION TO MONEY, you have also inherited your benefactor's income tax bill. Every dollar you inherit from a retirement savings plan or account is subject to federal, and generally speaking, state income tax. Don't get carried away with the dollar signs without tallying up Uncle Sam's share. You'll report any and all amounts that you withdraw from the inherited account on IRS Form 1040 and pay income tax on it that same year.

If the estate of the deceased is valued at more than $1 million (an amount that will move higher in years subsequent to 2003), federal estate tax also will be due. However, any estate tax paid can be used as a credit against the income tax owed on retirement assets—even if you do not pay the tax yourself. If you don't withdraw all of the money at once, the estate tax deduction can be carried forward until it is used up. According to Ed Slott, a Rockville Centre, New York, CPA and national expert on IRAs, this is perhaps the single biggest tax oversight associated with retirement savings accounts. It can save hundreds of thousands of dollars on a sizeable inheritance.

WITHDRAWAL OPTIONS

IF THE RETIREMENT ACCOUNT you inherited is worth $20,000, you may look at it and see $12,000 in your pocket after you pay state and federal income tax of 40 percent—maybe more if you're in a lower tax bracket. But a $20,000 IRA, inherited at age 40 and earning 8 percent a year, could turn into $115,000 worth of income over the next thirty or more years, after which you would still have nearly $60,000 remaining in your account.

That's why you need to think about what your inheritance means to you before you touch a single dollar. If you take the IRS up on the option it offers to any designated beneficiary of a retirement account—to allow you to take minimum annual withdrawals over your life expectancy from your inherited account and to preserve its tax-deferred growth—you'll avoid paying the entire tax bill in a single year and you can turn even a modest inheritance into a tidy nest egg for your own retirement.

There are plenty of wrinkles and side roads to this general policy of withdrawing your inheritance over your life expectancy.

◆ **Life expectancy.** For starters, you'll need to find your life expectancy as determined by the Single Life Expectancy Table (see the table on the following page), which is used to determine life expectancy for inherited retirement assets. (This is not the same as the Uniform Lifetime Table, which governs withdrawals for account owners.) The table provides the data you'll need to calculate your required minimum withdrawals from an inherited account. From the first year and going forward, there's a specified calculation to determine how much you must withdraw. The tables spell it out for you.

◆ **What it means to be a designated beneficiary.** You need to understand the very specific definition that the IRS has in mind for the term *designated beneficiary*. In order to qualify as a designated beneficiary, you must have been named on the beneficiary form of the deceased. It's not enough to be named in the will or to be named by a state court of law. If the deceased failed to name a beneficiary on the account's beneficiary form, the IRS may rule that there was *no* designated beneficiary. Even if you are entitled to inherit the assets in the account, your options for withdrawals as a nondesignated beneficiary are limited. If the account owner died before commencing required minimum withdrawals, you will have no more than five years to take the money out. If the account owner died *after* commencing required minimum withdrawals, you can use the remaining life expectancy of the deceased account owner. There is no negotiation or leeway on this matter.

As a designated beneficiary, you may also have the right to name the person who will, in turn, inherit any money that is left in the account you inherited if you pass away

SINGLE LIFE EXPECTANCY TABLE FOR INHERITED IRAS

AGE	LIFE EXPECTANCY (IN YEARS)	AGE	LIFE EXPECTANCY (IN YEARS)	AGE	LIFE EXPECTANCY (IN YEARS)	AGE	LIFE EXPECTANCY (IN YEARS)
0	82.4	28	55.3	56	28.7	84	8.1
1	81.6	29	54.3	57	27.9	85	7.6
2	80.6	30	53.3	58	27.0	86	7.1
3	79.7	31	52.4	59	26.1	87	6.7
4	78.7	32	51.4	60	25.2	88	6.3
5	77.7	33	50.4	61	24.4	89	5.9
6	76.7	34	49.4	62	23.5	90	5.5
7	75.8	35	48.5	63	22.7	91	5.2
8	74.8	36	47.5	64	21.8	92	4.9
9	73.8	37	46.5	65	21.0	93	4.6
10	72.8	38	45.6	66	20.2	94	4.3
11	71.8	39	44.6	67	19.4	95	4.1
12	70.8	40	43.6	68	18.6	96	3.8
13	69.9	41	42.7	69	17.8	97	3.6
14	68.9	42	41.7	70	17.0	98	3.4
15	67.9	43	40.7	71	16.3	99	3.1
16	66.9	44	39.8	72	15.5	100	2.9
17	66.0	45	38.8	73	14.8	101	2.7
18	65.0	46	37.9	74	14.1	102	2.5
19	64.0	47	37.0	75	13.4	103	2.3
20	63.0	48	36.0	76	12.7	104	2.1
21	62.1	49	35.1	77	12.1	105	1.9
22	61.1	50	34.2	78	11.4	106	1.7
23	60.1	51	33.3	79	10.8	107	1.5
24	59.1	52	32.3	80	10.2	108	1.4
25	58.2	53	31.4	81	9.7	109	1.2
26	57.2	54	30.5	82	9.1	110	1.1
27	56.2	55	29.6	83	8.6	111+	1.0

SOURCE: INTERNAL REVENUE SERVICE

before it is gone. That is, unless the original IRA owner has specifically named secondary beneficiaries in a customized beneficiary form. (You'll have to check the form yourself.)

Some investment companies have dragged their feet on this matter and balked when beneficiaries tried to take this action. But now that the IRS has made it clear in **NEW RULES** finalized in 2002 that a beneficiary has the right to name his or her own beneficiaries, many companies have fallen into line.

Don't think this is a way to get yet another lifetime of withdrawals from a single account. Any beneficiary that you designate would merely continue to use your remaining life expectancy to withdraw the balance of the account. This would also be true if you, the account's designated beneficiary, died during the period between the account owner's death and the following September 30th, the date by which a beneficiary must be finalized. Your successor beneficiary would have to use your life expectancy for calculating minimum withdrawals.

◆ **A timetable to sort out beneficiary issues.** If you are one of multiple beneficiaries, there is a window of opportunity to do some additional planning in the months after the death of the retirement account owner that can work in favor of all the beneficiaries. You have until September 30 of the year after the date of death to sort out any beneficiary issues. Here's what that means:

If, as in the example above, you and your sister inherit your father's IRA, you can split it in two and each of you can use your own personal life expectancies to determine a rate of withdrawal from the account. That way, your sister, who is ten years younger, has the option of taking lower annual withdrawals and spreading them over additional years. Or, if your father named you, your sister, and his church as equal beneficiaries, you can split the account three ways and pay off the church, and each of you can take withdrawals over your individual life expectancies.

You can disclaim your inheritance and make way for a younger beneficiary, who could get more benefit from the account by stretching its withdrawals over more years. Why would you do that? Let's say your father left his IRA to you, age 55, and your 20-year -old daughter. If you don't need the money, you can disclaim your amount, and your daughter can take withdrawals over her own life expectancy. It's simply a way to get more value out of the inherited IRA.

One more thing: If you are older than the deceased, and the deceased had already started to take **REQUIRED MINIMUM DISTRIBUTIONS** from the account you inherited, you can use the deceased's remaining life expectancy rather your own. For example, if the account owner died at age 72, with a life expectancy according to the new Uniform Lifetime Table, of 25.6 years, and you are 75, with a life expectancy from the Single Life Expectancy Table of 13.4 years, you can just about cut your minimum required withdrawals in half.

Why is all of this stuff about life expectancies and withdrawals such a big deal? Because the longer you put off withdrawals, and the more years over which you stretch withdrawals, the more value you can squeeze out of an inherited retirement account. The ratio of inherited value to total lifetime value of an account is mind-boggling. How about 10 or 20 to 1—or more? And that's with relatively modest investment returns. Bottom line: Stretch out—don't cash out—an inherited retirement account.

♦ **Beneficiary under the old rules.** If you inherited retirement assets before 2002, you may be taking withdrawals under **OLD IRS RULES** and you may be able to wring more years of **TAX-DEFERRED** growth by switching to the new rules. Or, if you were entitled to a five-year window to withdraw everything from the account you inherited, you may be able to go back and take withdrawals for the years that have passed and switch to the new rules to keep the account alive over your life expectancy.

♦ **Renaming the account.** Whatever you do, do not transfer the account you inherit into your own name. It will trigger an immediate tax bill and gone forever will be your opportunity to stretch your inheritance out to enjoy tax-deferred growth for years to come.

This is a huge issue, and it's easy to make a mistake if you are working with a financial professional who is inexperienced in these matters. According to Slott, many mistakes are made carelessly when a beneficiary decides to make a change to the account's investments or to transfer it to another financial institution. Before you do anything, you should retitle the account to reflect yourself as beneficiary but to retain the name of the deceased on the account. Here's the language recommended by knowledgeable accountants for retitling an inherited account: "Greta Good [name of the deceased], deceased, inherited IRA for the benefit of Sorta Good [name of the designated beneficiary], beneficiary, 000-00-0000 [Social Security number]."

A CHECKLIST FOR INHERITED RETIREMENT ASSETS

◆ Ask for a copy of the account owner's beneficiary form.

◆ If you are one of several beneficiaries, consider creating separate accounts.

◆ Consider disclaiming an account if (1) you don't need the money and (2) it has greater potential value if turned over to another designated or contingent beneficiary.

◆ Consult the Single Life Expectancy Table for inherited IRAs to determine the amount of your first and subsequent annual minimum required withdrawal.

◆ Retitle the account to include your name as beneficiary.

◆ Name a successor beneficiary, unless the original account owner has done so.

◆ If the deceased account owner was required to take a minimum withdrawal in the year of death, be sure to take it.

◆ Take *your* first withdrawal by December 31 of the year after the account owner's death.

◆ Take a deduction from income tax for any estate tax paid on the inherited account.

◆ If you are the spouse of the account owner and the sole beneficiary, consider a rollover to an account in your own name.

◆ If you are a spousal beneficiary under age 59 $\frac{1}{2}$, review your immediate income needs before rolling over to an account in your own name.

SPOUSES ARE DIFFERENT

IF YOU ARE A SPOUSE, and the **SOLE BENEFICIARY** of the account, you get special treatment. You have the option of **TRANSFERRING** the account you inherit to your own name and treating it as your own. Then, you can change your investment mix, name your own beneficiaries, and postpone withdrawals until you turn age 70½.

However, if you need access to the money you inherited for income and you are younger than age 59½, you may not want to put the account in your name because any money you withdraw would then be subject to a 10 percent early withdrawal penalty.

If you need access to the money you inherited and you are younger than 59½, you can do one of two things. You can keep the account in the name of the deceased and take the withdrawals you need—as long as they meet the minimum required for your own life expectancy. Or you can split the account. Keep enough in the account of your deceased spouse to generate the income you need through age 59½. Transfer the balance into an account in your own name.

In order to preserve your options, it's important to take any required minimum withdrawal for the year of your spouse's death if it hasn't been taken. If you don't take a required minimum withdrawal in the year of your spouse's death, the IRS will assume that the IRA has been rolled over to your name and any access you hoped to have to penalty-free income before age 59½ goes out the window. These guys are *picky*.

ROTH IRAS ARE DIFFERENT, TOO

THE RULES THAT GOVERN beneficiaries, including life expectancy tables and advice about how to retitle an inherited account, also apply to Roth IRAs. A Roth IRA account owner is not required to take any withdrawals in his or her lifetime. However, beneficiaries are required to follow the rules for required minimum withdrawals over their life expectancies. And they are subject to the same 50 percent penalty for not taking a required distribution that applies to traditional IRAs. The money they withdraw is entirely tax free, which may make it more attractive to withdraw all the money at once. But tax free means that any future earnings are also tax free. And that is a good reason to keep the account going.

Geez! This gets complicated. And these guidelines hit only the high points. There are plenty of niggling nuances about which the IRS is almost certain to have an opinion. If you inherit retirement assets, make sure you work with an accountant who is knowledgeable about inherited accounts. And take advantage of the free help offered by Ed Slott at www.irahelp.com. His panel of experts answers questions, and answers are archived on his site. It is simply the best.

Your Retirement Assets as Part of Your Estate

A proper beneficiary form is essential, and a trust may help you accomplish special goals.

IF YOUR DREAM is to leave some or most of your retirement savings to your heirs, it's important to make sure that the **TRANSFER** process is as smooth as possible. You should discuss your specific goals with an estate planning attorney, who can recommend strategies to achieve them. This section will help you organize your discussion.

Even if you plan on withdrawing every last penny of your retirement savings, you need to think about what will happen if your life is cut short—or if your investments do so well that you create an estate without even trying. As you think about your retirement assets as part of your estate, you should keep these basic concepts in mind:

◆ **Your beneficiary form is the will for your retirement savings.** Keep it up to date and file it with your will. The assets in your retirement accounts pass directly to your **DESIGNATED BENEFICIARIES**. They won't be subject to probate unless you fail to name a designated beneficiary on an approved beneficiary form.

If there are any surprises in your choice of beneficiaries, it may be hard to think about discussing them with your heirs. But it is a good idea to inform your beneficiaries that they have been designated and to make sure they understand the basics laid out in Number 24 about inheriting retirement savings.

◆ **If your retirement assets are sizeable, you should also consider a customized beneficiary form.** According to Kenneth

Brier, a Boston attorney who specializes in retirement and estate planning matters, a customized form is the only way to ensure that all contingencies are covered. For example, what happens to your retirement assets if your primary **BENEFICIARY** dies before withdrawing all of the money? Do you want to be able to name **CONTINGENT BENEFICIA-RIES** for that possibility? Do you want to make sure that your beneficiary can name his or her own beneficiaries? By covering all reasonable eventualities, you will go a long way in keeping peace among your heirs, always a challenge when a lot of money is at stake.

◆ **A Roth IRA is a simple estate planning strategy for mini-mizing the taxes your beneficiaries will pay.** If the value of your estate is less than the amount that you can pass on free of federal estate tax ($1 million in 2003, an amount that is scheduled to rise to $3.5 million in 2010), a Roth IRA **CONVERSION** can be a precious gift to your heirs. There's no deadline on a Roth IRA conversion, although there are eligibility rules: You can't convert an amount that you are required to take as a minimum **DISTRIBUTION**. And you can't convert at all if your income for the year exceeds $100,000. Until 2005, any minimum distribution you are required to take counts toward the $100,000 eligi-bility amount. So, it's a good idea to weigh a conversion strategy before you are 70½, when you'll be required to begin minimum distributions from your IRAs and most other tax-advantaged savings accounts.

◆ **A life insurance trust can maximize wealth transfer for a large estate.** One reason accountants have heralded the recent change in IRS rules that govern withdrawals from retirement accounts is that they generally allow for lower **REQUIRED MINIMUM DISTRIBUTIONS**—and that means a lower annual income tax bill. However, if your estate is large enough so that a sizable portion will be subject to federal estate tax (which starts at 37 percent and rises to a maximum of 50 percent in 2003), in addition to income tax, you may do better by your heirs if you withdraw enough each year to pay the premiums on a life insurance policy that is sized to pay your estate tax, thereby leaving more of your wealth to pass on to your heirs.

Here's how this strategy works: Say you have an estate that is worth $4 million, half of which is in an IRA. If you do nothing, your designated beneficiaries—your son and daughter, ages 35 and 40—would owe federal estate tax of around $1.4 million, based on 2003 estate tax rates and exclusion amounts. They would owe approximately $800,000 in federal and state income tax, figured at a combined 40 percent, on the $2 million IRA. However, that would be a wash after subtracting a credit for the estate tax paid—and then some. Here's a likely calculation:

Estate value	$4 million
Lifetime estate tax exclusion amount	$1 million
Federal estate tax due	$1.4 million
Income tax due on $2 million IRA	
at 40 percent	$800,000
	(offset by estate tax credit)
Total Inheritance	**$2.6 million**

Now, here's what you could accomplish with a life insurance trust based on figures supplied by Seth Medalie, CLU, ChFC, and president of the Bulfinch Group in suburban Boston and based on the life expectancy of a healthy male age 65. If you withdraw approximately $16,500 each year from your IRA and use it to purchase a $1.5 million whole life insurance policy, which is placed in an **IRREVOCABLE LIFE INSURANCE TRUST**, you reduce the amount of your IRA by the amount of your annual withdrawal, which is pretty much in line with what you'll be required to take as a minimum distribution after age 70½. However, with the money available from the life insurance trust to pay your federal estate tax bill, your heirs come out way ahead.

According to Ed Slott, the Rockville Centre, New York, CPA, this is a no-brainer strategy for individuals with significant estates and sizable IRAs. However, it's still hard to grasp the notion that you really can't take it with you, and simple denial keeps a lot of families from benefiting from this strategy.

TRUSTS TO ACHIEVE OTHER GOALS

TRUSTS ARE NOT an ideal place, in general, for retirement savings—they can be inflexible, especially when it comes to taxes. However, they work well in situations where you have a very specific goal. For example, if you are a single parent and your young adult children are your intended beneficiaries, a revocable trust that becomes irrevocable upon your death and funded with your retirement savings can take the pressure off decisions that your kids could be unprepared to make. You can put your retirement savings in a revocable trust, name an executor who can make sure that your eighteen-year-old doesn't take a big withdrawal, unaware of the income tax implications, or fails to take a required minimum distribution, simply because he didn't know he should. Once your children are at an age where you feel they are ready to shoulder the responsibility of a sizable inheritance, you can dissolve the trust.

A marital trust is also a useful option if you are on a second or third marriage and you want to provide a source of income for your current spouse, but you also want to ensure that your retirement savings are passed on to your children from your first marriage. Just remember that income from a marital trust must be paid out annually, so your spouse won't have the option of postponing taxable income into the future.

IF YOU ARE CHARITABLY INCLINED

ONE WAY TO AVOID the onerous income tax on your retirement savings is to bequeath some or all of it to charity. That process has actually gotten easier under **NEW IRS RULES** that govern distributions from retirement plans. You can name a charity as a beneficiary along with other individuals—family members or friends—and everyone can make out okay. A charity can inherit some of your retirement savings tax-free and other beneficiaries can preserve the right to take withdrawals over their individual life expectancies. You couldn't do that under the **OLD RULES**. Naming a charity as your beneficiary along with individuals would have forced everyone to take an immediate withdrawal because a charity has no life expectancy.

That said, it's not a good idea to give your retirement savings away to a charitable cause in your lifetime. The IRS will take the position that *you* have taken a distribution in order to give your money away. You'll end up with an income tax bill and the charity will end up with less.

As always, when you have a sizable estate, it's important to work these matters through with an estate planning professional. It's important to understand something about your options. But estate planning is not a do-it-yourself proposition. There's simply too much at stake.

IF YOU PLAN TO PASS ON YOUR COMPANY STOCK

IF YOU TOOK a **LUMP SUM DISTRIBUTION** of your employer's stock, **IN KIND**, and paid income tax on the **COST BASIS** so that you could lower the tax bill on the **NET UNREALIZED APPRECIATION (NUA)**, you can pass this tax benefit on to your heirs. If these securities are part of your estate, your beneficiaries will have to pay **CAPITAL GAINS** tax on the NUA, but they will receive a **STEP-UP** in cost basis to market value. And, they will also inherit any other special tax opportunities that would have been accorded to you. For example, if you were entitled to use special **TEN-YEAR FORWARD AVERAGING** tax computation, your beneficiaries are entitled to use it, too. This gets too complicated to generalize. If you inherit employer stock, get tax and financial advice that applies to your specific situation.

SOME FINAL THOUGHTS

PERHAPS THE BIGGEST challenge associated with retirement savings that are destined for your heirs is that you are traveling into uncharted territory. Retirement savings plans were designed for accumulation, and in writing regulations both Congress and the IRS focused primarily on how the money would get into the plans, how fast it went in, and how much ended up there. It was only when people realized that millions of dollars have accumulated in individual plans that serious attention was focused on what happens when the money flows out. Although the IRS has gone a long way to help make this process simpler for both account owners and beneficiaries with a new set of regulations, it is unlikely to be its last word on the subject.

The attention you pay to your retirement assets should be proportionate to their value. That's just good common sense, something that has been in short supply over the years among those who have written the rules as well as those who are left to interpret them.

"What were they thinking?" you might ask yourself when you start talking about customized beneficiary forms, life insurance trusts, and Roth IRAs with your financial adviser. An even more important question for you to ponder is "what will they think of next?"

Glossary

after-tax dollars. A retirement savings account contribution that comes from money on which you have already paid income tax.

annuity units. A portion of an annuity, similar to a mutual fund share, that is used to calculate payments on a variable income annuity contract.

applicable distribution period (ADP). Your life expectancy from the Uniform Lifetime Table or the Joint and Last Survivor Expectancy Table, used as a divisor to figure your required minimum distribution amount.

asset allocation. Dividing your investments among different types of assets, such as stocks, bonds, and cash, for the purpose of minimizing risk.

benchmark rate of return. Rate of interest that an insurance company uses to determine the payments on a variable annuity contract. Also known as the *assumed interest rate*.

beneficiary. The person you name to receive your assets upon your death.

capital gain. The difference between an asset's cost basis and selling price when the difference is positive.

cash balance pension plan. A type of workplace retirement plan that combines the guaranteed benefit of a traditional pension with the portability of a defined contribution plan. Employers create individual accounts for each employee and credit them with a dollar amount each year based on projected account values at retirement.

contingent beneficiary. The person you name to receive your assets upon your death if the primary beneficiary is unable to do so, because of death, for example, or because the primary beneficiary disclaims them.

conversion. The process of rolling over traditional IRA assets into a Roth IRA without penalty. However, income tax is due on the rollover amount.

cost basis. The amount treated as the purchase price or cost of an asset for the purpose of figuring a taxable gain or loss when it's sold. Also known as *basis*.

custodial services. Legal responsibility for management and safekeeping of assets.

defined benefit plan. A type of pension plan that specifies both the amount and the timing of the benefit as well as a formula for calculating it.

defined contribution plan. A type of workplace retirement plan that specifies how much employee and employer can contribute, how contributions are made, and when they are made.

designated beneficiary. The IRS definition of a recognized beneficiary of a retirement plan. Must be a "natural person" or a qualified trust as opposed to an entity such as a charity or a corporation.

direct rollover. A direct transfer of funds directly from one retirement plan into another without incurring taxes or penalty.

distribution. A payout from a tax-advantaged retirement account.

domestic partnership agreement. A written agreement that spells out details of the finances between two unmarried partners, such as division of ownership of accounts, tangible items, and real estate. To stand up in court, the agreement should be drafted by an attorney and reviewed by the attorneys of both parties to the agreement.

Employee Stock Ownership Plan (ESOP). A type of workplace retirement savings plan that is funded primarily— or even exclusively—with shares of the company's common stock.

employer match. An employer's contribution to an employee's retirement savings account, typically between 1 percent and 5 percent.

expense ratio. The amount, expressed as a percentage of total investment, that shareholders pay annually for mutual fund operating expenses and management fees.

financial supermarket. A company that offers a wide range of financial services including individual securities, mutual funds, cash management, asset management, insurance, and check writing.

fixed income annuity. A series of fixed payments guaranteed to last until your death, or the death of a joint beneficiary, or over a specific time period, such as ten to twenty years.

floor plan. Also called a *floor-offset plan*. Another type of hybrid pension plan with both defined benefit and defined contribution characteristics. The plan establishes a minimum benefit level which can be exceeded but not diminished.

grandfathered. Exempted from a new law and allowed to use terms and conditions of a previous law.

growth. Investment style that targets the stock of companies that are expected to grow faster than the market's average growth rate.

in kind. Of the same type; for example, a stock that is taken from a retirement account "in kind" is not sold. It is withdrawn as it is.

income annuity. A series of fixed or variable payments guaranteed to last until death, or over a specific time period, such as ten or twenty years. Other types of annuities can be used to accumulate savings.

irrevocable life insurance trust. A trust that is designed to hold a life insurance policy and which cannot be changed or terminated by the person who created it.

laddered. Refers to a portfolio of individual bonds where maturities have been staggered to come due at different times.

life annuity. An income annuity that guarantees income payments, at least annually, over your entire lifetime.

life estate. A legal freehold interest in land or real estate limited by the life of the person holding it.

load. Sales charge paid by an investor who buys shares in a mutual fund or annuity. Loads may be charged when shares or units are purchased or when they are sold, in which case they may be referred to as *back-end loads*. A fund that does not charge a load is called a *no-load fund*.

lump sum distribution. A distribution of the entire balance of all qualified plans of a similar type taken in one taxable year.

maturity date. The date on which the issuer of a bond agrees to repay the principal to the buyer.

minimum distribution allowance. The portion of a lump sum distribution of less than $70,000 that is not taxed. That amount is the smaller of $10,000 or half of the entire distribution, minus 20 percent of the amount of the distribution over $20,000.

net unrealized appreciation (NUA). The amount by which an asset has increased in value and on which taxes have not yet been paid because the asset has been transferred from one type of retirement account to another but has not been sold.

new IRS rules. Final regulations governing required distributions from retirement plans, proposed in 2001, finalized in 2002, with an effective date of January 1, 2003.

nonqualified plan. Any workplace retirement plan that does not fall under the jurisdiction of the Employment Retirement Income Security Act of 1974.

old IRS rules. Proposed rules that were issued in 1987 and never finalized, which governed required distributions from retirement plans until 2001.

ordinary income. Income that does not qualify for special tax treatment, such as wages earned or dividends and interest paid on an investment.

pension equity plan. Another type of hybrid pension plan that defines benefits in terms of a current lump sum value instead of an annuity payable on retirement.

plan document. A required, official written description of the policies and procedures of a qualified workplace retirement savings plan.

profit sharing plan. A type of workplace retirement plan that allows employers to make annual contributions at their discretion, regardless of profitability.

Qualified Domestic Relations Order (QDRO). A court-approved order that allows divorcing couples to divide assets in a qualified retirement plan without incurring a penalty or immediate taxes.

qualified plan. Any workplace retirement plan that qualifies for favorable tax treatment under section 401 of the U.S. Tax Code and falls under the jurisdiction of the Employment Retirement Income Security Act of 1974.

rebalancing. Shifting money between investments to restore the proportions of the desired mix of assets in your portfolio.

recharacterizing. Converting assets from a Roth IRA back to a traditional IRA to correct an error or to capture a more favorable tax situation.

required beginning date. The deadline for taking your first required minimum distribution from most tax-advantaged savings plans or accounts.

required minimum distribution. An amount that the IRS requires you to withdraw from your tax-advantaged retirement savings plans after age 70½.

restricted stock. A stock that is not registered by the Securities and Exchange Commission (SEC) and not sold publicly.

roll over. To receive assets from one retirement plan and transfer them to another.

sole beneficiary. The only primary beneficiary named.

step-up. A term that applies to the cost basis of an inherited asset. For the purpose of determining future taxes, an asset is valued at the current market price rather than what was paid for it by the deceased.

substantially equal payments. An IRS-approved plan for withdrawing assets from a tax-advantaged account without penalty regardless of the individual's age. The IRS accepts three formulas for calculating the stream of income.

systematic withdrawal plan. An option that allows you to withdraw your money from a former employer's tax-deferred retirement plan in a stream of fixed periodic payments.

tax deductible. When used in reference to retirement savings, a contribution that generates a tax deduction.

tax deferred. An investment whose earnings accumulate free of taxes until the investor takes possession of them.

tax-deferred annuity. An annuity that is used to accumulate savings on which taxes on earnings are deferred until the money is withdrawn by the annuity owner.

ten-year forward averaging. A method of computing taxes on a lump sum distribution from a qualified retirement plan as though the distribution were spread over a ten-year period.

term certain annuity. An income annuity that guarantees income payments over a specified period of time, expressed in years.

transfer. The movement of a tax-advantaged account from one custodian to another without tax or penalty.

unlimited marital deduction. The ability for one spouse to pass on unlimited amount of money or property to a spouse who is an American citizen.

value. Investment style that targets the stock of companies that have lost favor with investors, but appear to have the potential to turn around.

variable annuity. A type of annuity, either for income or accumulation, where the return varies in accordance with the investment performance of portfolios selected by the annuity owner.

variable income annuity. A series of variable payments guaranteed to last until death, or the death of a joint beneficiary, or over a specific time period, such as ten to twenty years.

vested. Eligible to claim your retirement benefits upon separation from service.

Windfall Elimination Provision. A Social Security provision that eliminates or reduces benefit payments to someone who is covered by a retirement system outside of Social Security and also made payments to Social Security.

INDEX

ABOUT BLOOMBERG

Bloomberg L.P., founded in 1981, is a global information services, news, and media company. Headquartered in New York, the company has nine sales offices, two data centers, and 87 news bureaus worldwide.

Bloomberg, serving customers in 126 countries around the world, holds a unique position within the financial services industry by providing an unparalleled range of features in a single package known as the BLOOMBERG PROFESSIONAL® service. By addressing the demand for investment performance and efficiency through an exceptional combination of information, analytic, electronic trading, and Straight Through Processing tools, Bloomberg has built a worldwide customer base of corporations, issuers, financial intermediaries, and institutional investors.

BLOOMBERG NEWS®, founded in 1990, provides stories and columns on business, general news, politics, and sports to leading newspapers and magazines throughout the world. BLOOMBERG TELEVISION®, a 24-hour business and financial news network, is produced and distributed globally in seven different languages. BLOOMBERG RADIO℠ is an international radio network anchored by flagship station BLOOMBERG® WBBR 1130 in New York.

In addition to the BLOOMBERG PRESS® line of books, Bloomberg publishes *BLOOMBERG MARKETS*™, *BLOOMBERG PERSONAL FINANCE*®, and *BLOOMBERG WEALTH MANAGER*®. To learn more about Bloomberg, call a sales representative at:

Frankfurt:	49-69-92041-280	São Paulo:	5511-3048-4506
Hong Kong:	852-2977-6900	Singapore:	65-6212-1100
London:	44-20-7330-7500	Sydney:	612-9777-8686
New York:	1-212-318-2200	Tokyo:	813-3201-8910
San Francisco:	1-415-912-2970		

ABOUT THE AUTHOR

Margaret (Peggy) A. Malaspina is principal of Malaspina Communications, a Massachusetts-based agency that specializes in shareholder, adviser, corporate, and marketing communications for some of the nation's largest investment companies. A former vice president at Fidelity Investments, Malaspina has twenty years of experience in the financial services industry. She helped forge Fidelity's corporate communications strategies in the early 1980s. She created the firm's book publishing venture, launched the writing career of fund-manager-turned-best-selling-author Peter Lynch, and was part of the executive management team that started *Worth* magazine. Malaspina is the author of *Don't Die Broke,* the first comprehensive lay-person's guide to taking money out of today's retirement and pension plans. She is a frequent guest on radio and television financial shows and a frequent speaker at professional investment conferences. She lives and works near Boston.